CUBA'S HEALTH CARE SYSTEM
WHERE HUMANITY COMES FIRST

CUBA'S HEALTH CARE SYSTEM
WHERE HUMANITY COMES FIRST

ELLEN BERNSTEIN
WITH INTRODUCTION BY REV. LUCIUS WALKER, JR.

battle of ideas press
vancouver

A Battle of Ideas Press Publication
First Edition, September 2010

Library and Archives Canada Cataloguing in Publication

Bernstein, Ellen, 1952-
    Health care in Cuba : where humanity comes first / Ellen
Bernstein ; editor, Ali Yerevani.

ISBN 978-0-9864716-2-9

1. Medical care--Cuba. I. Title.

RA456.C7B47 2010   362.1097291   C2010-904143-7

Cover Photos: *Background photo - Logo of Cuba's Ministry of Public
Health. Clockwise from top left: Cuban medical team in Pakistan after 2006
earthquake; Cuban doctor volunteering in Pakistan; Students from the Latin
American School of Medicine in 2009 May Day March in Havana, Cuba;
Medical Clinic in Havana, Cuba. Quote on the wall from Che Guevara,
"The life of a human being is worth more than all the gold of the world's
richest man."*

Printed and manufactured in Canada
Printed by Gramma Publications
Vancouver, British Columbia, Canada

Battle of Ideas Press
PO Box 21607
Vancouver, BC
V5L 5G3
Canada

battle of ideas press
www.battleofideaspress.com
info@battleofideaspress.com

Battle of Ideas Press
is a publisher that reflects the conflicting ideas that are shaping the political, economic, social and psychological setup of our world today from the standpoint of working and oppressed people. We intend to present an alternative that is intellectually honest and presents facts, figures and analysis for those who are interested to know the truth and want to change the world to a better place.

CONTENTS

Foreword..15

Introduction..19

Health Care in Cuba: Where Humanity Comes First
by Ellen Bernstein

1. *A Health Care System that Works*..*25*

2. *The US Blockade Attacks Cuba's Health Care System*..............*39*

3. *Internationalism: A Proud Tradition of Cuban
   Health Care*..*51*

4. *Striving for Perfection: New Developments in Cuban
   Health Care*..*57*

5. *An Inspiration to the World*..*61*

PHOTOS

APPENDIX

*Speech by Fidel Castro to the First Graduating Class of the
   Latin American School of Medicine*..................................*87*

Cuba Answers the Call for Doctors...101

Cuba's Health Care Revolution: 30 Years On...............................109

Health-Workforce Development in the Cuban
      Health System..115

The Right to Health in Times of Economic Crisis:
      Cuba's Way..121

Role of the USA in Shortage of Food and Medicine in Cuba.......127

MAPS

Map of Cuba...142

Map of Cuba, the Caribbean and the Americas..............144

Nations Where Cuba Offered Health Assistance
in 2002...146

Nations That Have Students Studying in Cuba
at the Latin American School of Medicine (ELAM).......148

*Dedicated to health and healing in Cuba and
throughout the world*

Ellen Bernstein has served as Associate Director of the Interreligious Foundation for Community Organization (IFCO) since 2003. She joined the staff of IFCO in 1992, and previously held the title of Grants Administrator. She has been a key staff member of IFCO's project Pastors for Peace, and has been deeply and integrally involved in IFCO's historic work with Cuba.

Ellen has been a leader of more than 60 trips to Cuba since 1993. She has also organized 18 Congressional delegations, and traveled to Cuba with 19 members of Congress and 40 key Congressional aides. She has worked closely with IFCO's director and attorneys to successfully defend IFCO against a variety of US government challenges. She also had a leadership role in the national grassroots campaign to return Elián González to his father in Cuba. As IFCO's grants administrator, Ellen has worked directly with the dozens of domestic grassroots community projects for which IFCO serves as fiscal sponsor.

Ellen is a doctoral candidate in counseling psychology at Columbia University Teachers College, and a graduate of Princeton University (BA, psychology, 1973). Before joining the staff of IFCO, she worked for 10 years as a psychotherapist in Oberlin, Ohio.

FOREWORD
Tamara Hansen

"A miracle" and "amazing", you hear these words frequently from many people who travel to Cuba and have come in touch with the Cuban healthcare system, either directly themselves or by observing how the Cuban medical system works in practice. Significant numbers of healthcare professionals, medical scientists and researchers have done a superb job in analyzing and explaining the success of Cuba's healthcare system. Mostly, they tell us how efficient the system is and of its important focus on preventive medicine rather than curative medicine. They hold Cuba up as an example. The same medical and scientific community explains to us that Cuba not only has efficient healthcare management, but that this system is based on free care for all. At the same time, it promotes medical and preventive care at the community level and insures healthy living for each Cuban by having doctors and healthcare professionals follow individual's wellbeing on a regular basis. Without these principals how could a third world country with only 11 and a half million people achieve such huge monumental successes in all fields of medical sciences including health care, medical training and education, medical planning and management, as well as pharmaceutical research and production.

Incredibly many of these documents fail to spot the most important disadvantage Cuba has in comparison with all other Latin American countries. They forget to include the undeniable fact that the Cuban people and government are working under a severe, inhuman and criminal blockade imposed by the United States government for 50 years. For us, outside of Cuba, maintaining the blockade is a clear case of moral failure of all US administrations since the 1959 Cuban Revolution. However, for the people of Cuba and their revolutionary government this blockade translates into a huge loss of money - billions of dollars – as well as negative and harmful consequences on all aspects of life in Cuba, including medical care.

Progressing in health care regardless of the devastating aspects of the US blockade could not be possible without the social and political consciousness of the Cuban people combined with their tremendous energy, enthusiasm and willpower. All of Cuba's remarkable achievements should be understood within this political context, even more so because in the height of the Special Period from 1989 to 1993, Cuba's economy shrunk by 35% and its foreign trade was cut by 85% as a result of the collapse of the Soviet Union and socialist bloc. During this same period Cuba lost 70% of the resources used to provide medical equipment and supplies. The magnitude of Cuba's successful progress can only be fully appreciated when you add the impact of the US blockade of Cuba during that period of time and the fact that the blockade was strengthened with the Torricelli Law of 1992 and the Helms-Burton Act of 1996.

As a result of this knowledge the question comes back again: How did a third world country, with such limited resources, achieve its exemplary progress not only domestically but also export it to other third world countries? How did it become a leader for the rest of the world? How does it provide these services both inside and outside of Cuba basically for free? Certainly, one can dig into the mechanisms of Cuban health care to find the answer. However, the fundamental truth lies not within the technical aspects of Cuba's healthcare system, but with the political and philosophical foundation of the Cuban government. In Cuba, state power, which roots itself in the victorious Cuban Revolution of 1959 and the proclamation of its socialist nature and socialist project, plays a vital role in implementing and preserving the humanist base of the healthcare system. A system that plans, functions and prioritizes human needs and not profit, a healthcare system where humanity comes first. In

Cuba, humanity and human rights are the same.

This book in your hands is divided in two sections. The first section is an analysis of the Cuban healthcare system with the finest scientific method used by Ellen Bernstein, one of the leading researchers on Cuba's healthcare system. This section could be called, if you will, Cuba 101: health care education for everyone. It is comprehensive, simple and to the point. It contains all you really need to know about a healthcare system that puts humanity first, which is working so well for all Cubans. The second part, the appendix, starts with a speech by Fidel Castro, which is an explanation of Cuba's approach to health care as a foundation to upholding human rights and revolutionary internationalism. The next two documents are taken from the United Nations' World Health Organization (WHO). The WHO is the directing and coordinating authority for international health within the United Nations' system. The last three articles are taken with permission from the Lancet. The Lancet is one of the world's leading authoritative medical journals and is widely used as an independent and reliable source in the research and scientific community, as well as international media. Needless to say we added the appendix section for your further information and documentation to support the valuable first section by Ellen Bernstein. We hope this book will become part of understanding the leadership role Cuba's example can play in promoting universal access to healthcare for people all over the world.

Tamara Hansen was the co-chair from 2008-10, and executive committee member from 2006-10, of the Canadian Network on Cuba (CNC). Currently she is the coordinator of Vancouver Communities in Solidarity with Cuba (VCSC). She was also the national coordinator of the Ernesto Che Guevara Volunteer Work Brigade to Cuba 2009-10. Tamara is the author of the new book "5 Decades of the Cuban Revolution: Challenges of an Unwavering Leadership" published by Battle of Ideas Press in April 2010.

INTRODUCTION
*Rev. Lucius Walker, Jr.**

For decades there has been a need for a practical and factual overview of the unique health care system of Cuba. This need is evidenced by the numerous requests our office receives for information about health care in Cuba. In my view no one is more qualified to write this overview then Ellen Bernstein, Associate Director of IFCO/Pastors for Peace. Bernstein's years of study and close observation of the Cuban health care system is reflected in the following pages.

In the face of daunting costs of health insurance and pharmaceuticals in the United States, it is refreshing and encouraging to read the story of Cuba's health care accomplishments in spite of its shortages. Cuba has demonstrated what is possible to achieve if there is a political will to make health care a national priority and a basic human right rather than a business.

With ease Bernstein moves us from the local family doctors in the neighborhood clinics to polyclinics, to Cuba's network of hospitals, to the network of specialty care facilities and ultimately to Cuba's Bio-technological poll where cures are being discovered for diseases that plague not only Cuba but the world.

In the dozens of times that IFCO has been to Cuba with Friendshipment Caravans and delegations we have been able to observe first-hand the excellence of Cuban health care. Among others we have seen maternity wards, pediatric hospitals and general doctors offices and met the medical professionals that run the facilities as well as the patients. After this the question comes up, how does such a small island with only 11 and half million people have such a great health care system? The answer that comes to us is because unlike US, in Cuba human needs come first.

This book also gives a helpful overview of the U.S. Blockade which attacks the Cuban health care system and Cuba's commitment to "Internationalism" through which it provides health care to all parts of the world – including free medical training for students from 50 countries (even the United States). This program for free medical training at the Latin American School of Medicine is intended especially for those that come from communities of color and poor communities who would not traditionally have the opportunity to attend medical school in the US. In return for their scholarships, they agree to serve in medically underserved communities as doctors.

IFCO hopes that this book will be a major eye-opening contribution to those who want to know more about health care in Cuba as well as those who want to see a model of universal health care.

Rev. Lucius Walker, Jr.

August 2010

Rev. Lucius Walker, Jr. is the executive director of the Interreligious Foundation for Community Organization (IFCO)/Pastors for Peace. He served as Associate General Secretary of the National Council of Churches of Christ in the USA from 1973 through 1978. In January 1979, he returned to IFCO, which has the distinction of being the only national ecumenical foundation committed exclusively to the support of community organizing.

In 1988, Rev. Walker was shot and wounded in a attack by the US-backed contras on innocent civilians as he led an IFCO study delegation to Nicaragua's Atlantic Coast region. In response to the attack, Rev. Walker conceived the project Pastors for Peace, which organizes humanitarian aid caravans as a way to assist the victims of US foreign policy. IFCO/Pastors for Peace has delivered 60 national humanitarian aid caravans to Cuba, El Salvador, Guatemala, Honduras, Nicaragua, and Chiapas, Mexico. In 2005-6 it organized two emergency caravans to New Orleans and the Gulf Coast in the aftermath of Hurricane Katrina.

In January 1996, Rev. Walker was arrested by U.S. authorities because he dared to take computers to hospitals in Cuba. When the computers were seized, Rev. Walker and four others engaged in a "Fast for Life" until the computers were released. The fast lasted 94 days and resulted in the release of the computers which were delivered to Cuba in September of that same year. This action followed another fast for a Little Yellow School Bus, seized by US

Treasury on the way to Cuba on the Caravan in 1993. This fast lasted for 23 days and resulted in the release of the bus to Cuba.

Rev. Walker is the recipient of numerous honorary degrees and peace awards, including the Gandhi Peace Award and the Thomas Merton Award.

* Rev. Lucius Walker, Jr. passed away peacefully in September 2010, in his home in New York, after over 40 years of prophetic and visionary leadership.

Rev. Lucius Walker, Jr. speaking at the May Day Rally in Havana. May 1, 2003

A Health Care System That Works

>> Imagine: a health care system in which everyone is entitled to high quality health care, free of charge.

>> Imagine: a health care system in which there's a doctor for every 151 people — a family doctor and a nurse on call for every 120 families.

>> Imagine: a health care system in which all people — regardless of age, class, race, or location — are entitled to and receive the same level of care.

For those of us who struggle with health care issues in the United States, it might be hard to imagine that such a system could possibly exist — but it does exist, in the innovative health care program of our neighbour nation Cuba.

Cuba's system of community medicine, with its strong focus on universal primary and preventive care, is world renowned, and has received numerous awards from the United Nations and international health organizations. Cuba s health indicators are comparable to those of the world's most developed nations — and Cuba has continued to prioritize health care, even during the worst years of the US economic blockade. Cuba's family doctors and nurses have set a worldwide example since Cuba's community medicine program was implemented in 1984.

Cuba has the highest number of doctors per capita of any nation: 74,552 doctors in 2008. That's 66.2 doctors per 10,000 inhabitants; one doctor for every 151 people who live in Cuba. And more than 32,000 of Cuba's doctors are local family doctors who focus on primary care. What that means is that there is a doctor and a nurse in every neighbourhood of 120 families. If there are 120 families living in a high-rise apartment building then there's a doctor in that building. In an urban area or a smaller town, there's a doctor just a few blocks away - no matter what neighbourhood you're in. There are also doctors in day care centers, schools, workplaces, bus stations, etc. Family doctors and nurses have residence apartments where their offices are located; they rotate duty, so someone is always on call.

Cuban family doctors maintain preventive health records of all the people in their neighbourhood, so they know who might need extra care, or who hasn't had a booster shot or a check-up. And if you don't go to see the doctor, s/he'll go to your house to see you. In this way, the Cuban health care system assures that every expectant mother gets thorough prenatal care, that every child gets vaccinated, that every diabetic or asthmatic gets monitored. And family doctors and nurses can make ongoing interventions in areas, such as diet or smoking, that improve patients' lifestyles and life expectancies.

As any school of public health teaches, comprehensive primary care makes health systems more efficient and practical, prevents disease, and promotes healthy lifestyles. The Cuban Health Ministry describes its primary care system of family doctors and nurses as "the best strength and potential of our system which allows us to maintain our health indicators and meet our population's needs."

In the Cuban system, family doctors do front-line preventive care and maintenance for the whole population. When a patient needs lab tests or X-rays or more specialized treatment, s/he goes to the neighbourhood policlinic.

The policlinic system was established in 1974; there is one policlinic for every 25,000 people, in all parts of the country, urban or rural. A patient who needs more serious treatment — surgery or chemotherapy — gets referred from the policlinic to a hospital. Cuba has 265 hospitals with a total of 70,424 beds (1 for every 159 inhabitants); these include general, surgical, maternity, pediatric, psychiatric, orthopedic, rehabilitation and teaching hospitals.

In contrast to the US, where many uninsured patients get their only care in hospital emergency rooms, the availability of good universal primary care in Cuba helps to decrease the number of patients who need to be admitted to hospitals. Hospital admissions for nonemergency operations have also decreased because of the acute shortages of medicines, equipment, and medical supplies caused by the US economic blockade.

Cuba also has a number of intermediate programs which allow for special care without full hospitalization. Hogares maternos (maternity homes) allow for special care for pregnant women as they approach the end of their pregnancies, or if they have problems that need monitoring. Special treatment for the elderly is given in Hogares de abuelos (grandparents' homes).

All health services in Cuba are free of charge - everything from a well-baby check-up to an organ transplant. All Cubans receive health care services at no cost: no insurance, no co payments, no doctors' bills to pay — not for $10, not for $10,000.

Cuban families assume the cost of outpatient prescriptions, eyeglasses, hearing aids, dental and orthopedic prostheses, wheelchairs, crutches, canes, and walkers. Prices (in Cuban pesos) are subsidized to stay low.

Low-income people receive financial help, and receive their prescriptions free of charge. Facilities now charge fees for foreign patients who can pay for services such as plastic surgery or specialized treatments. The income from these patients is used to subsidize the free services which continue to be given to all Cubans — plus all the international service which Cuba gives free of charge to needy patients from Latin America, Africa, and the Ukraine and other parts of the world.

Statistics on Cuba's Successes
Health Indicators in Cuba: 2006

■ Infant mortality is 5.0/1,000 live births (among the 25 best in the world)*	■ 100 % of the population is covered by family doctors and nurses**
■ Maternal mortality is 3.0/10,000 live births	■ 99.9% of births take place in health care institutions with specialized personnel
■ 100% of Cuban children are vaccinated against 13 preventable diseases	■ Child mortality under the age of 5 is 7.0/1,000 live births (among the best in the world)
■ 95% of pregnant women are identified in their first trimester and receive 11 specialized medical consultations during each pregnancy	■ Life expectancy is 78 years of age. At 60, a Cuban can expect to live 19 years longer; at 80, a Cuban can expect to live 8 years longer
■ Illnesses such as tuberculosis and leptospirosis have been virtually eradicated, and Cuba remains cholera-free	■ The primary causes of death in Cuba are heart disease, cancer, stroke, and other diseases of the most developed nations

■ Diphtheria, infant tetanus, measles, malaria, poliomyelitis and other diseases have been eradicated in Cuba. Death by diarrhea has been reduced to the levels found in the most developed nations

*World Health Organization, 2006 **Infomed

Cuba's low infant mortality rate, which is only 5.0/1,000 live births, is recognized throughout the world as on a par with the most developed nations. By comparison, the infant mortality rate in Nicaragua in 1997 was twelve times as high – 29/1,000; in Haiti, it was 135/1,000; in Latin America, on average, 38/1,000; and even in the US it was slightly higher at 7/1,000. But US infant mortality statistics show enormous variability according to economic class factors. The US national average for African-American children is 14/1,000, and in inner city areas such as Harlem, infant mortality rates can approach 40-50/1,000. In contrast, Cuba's health statistics show a very even distribution — the statistics stay constant from the most urban to the most rural areas. Disease frequencies are also evenly distributed between urban, urban/rural, and rural areas — which shows that health care services in Cuba reach all levels of the population, in the country as well as the city.

Cuba has a universal program of vaccinations — which means that many common diseases, such as measles, malaria, German measles, and polio, have been eradicated in Cuba. Meningitis B&C, hepatitis B, encephalitis and leptospirosis vaccines recently developed in Cuba have also been enormously effective.

Health Care For Life

Life expectancy in Cuba was less than 65 in 1959; since the time of the revolution, it has been raised to 78 years of age. Try to imagine the personal and social significance of being able to increase everyone›s life expectancy 13 years in just two generations!

The principal causes of death in Cuba are the same as in the most developed nations. They include heart disease, cancer, stroke, accidents, influenza/pneumonia, circulatory diseases, diabetes, liver disease, and bronchitis/ emphysema/asthma. They do not include AIDS, childhood diarrhea, malnutrition, cholera, or other infectious diseases.

On The Cutting Edge Of Medical Innovations

Cuba is internationally known for its advances in biotechnology. Cuban scientists have developed unique treatments for some diseases which US doctors don't yet know how to cure — including *retinitis pigmentosa*, vitiligo, and meningitis. Cuba is on the cutting edge in the search for cures for the most recalcitrant diseases which plague our world today:

>> Cuban vaccines against several strains of AIDS are in clinical trials.

>> Cuba is testing seven different therapeutic vaccines against cancer — to shrink tumors and prevent relapses in patients who already have the disease.

>> Cuban research on epidermal growth factor and monoclonal antibodies have led to pioneering new approaches to cancer treatment, which mobilize the body's own immune system to fight cancer on a cellular level.

>> Cuba is conducting research on new vaccines against cholera, tuberculosis, hepatitis A & C, dengue fever, and AIDS.

>> Cuba is producing vaccines to protect its own population against 13 different diseases, including meningitis B & C, hepatitis B & C, leptospirosis, typhoid, measles, rubella, diphtheria, pertussis, and tetanus.

>> Cuba is working to produce medications which are too expensive to import (such as chemotherapy drugs and the 'triple cocktail' used for AIDS treatment), for its own population and in other developing nations with critical needs.

>> Cuban neuroscientists are working on early detection of Alzheimer's disease, detection of hearing loss in newborns (to guard against deficits in language and cognitive development), research on Parkinson's disease, etc.

Chronology Of Cuba's Vaccination Program (Granma, 3/5/99)

1960s:

1962: Vaccination against poliomyelitis and 'tetanus/

diphtheria/whooping cough.

1964: A permanent national vaccination program is initiated. Vaccination centers are

set up across the country, one center for every 30,000 inhabitants. Percentage of population immunized goes up to 60%, as promised.

1968-9: A national program funded by UNICEF and the Cuban Ministry of Health immunizes all Cubans under age 15 in rural areas for tetanus/diphtheria/ whooping cough and TB.

<u>**1970s:**</u>

1971: All children aged 6 months - 5 years are vaccinated against measles.

1974: New community policlinics are created, each covering a sector of about 30,000 inhabitants; immunization levels rise to 75-80%

1975: First national anti-tetanus vaccination campaign for women at home, where tetanus is most frequent. 98% of housewives are vaccinated.

1976: Booster doses of tetanus for housewives.

1979: In response to an increase in meningitis A&C, 3 million Cubans are immunized with a French vaccine.

<u>**1980s:**</u>

1980: A new vaccination program is elaborated, to

start administering anti-typhoid, diphtheria, and TB vaccines in the schools.

1982: A long-term strategy is introduced to protect girls against rubella (German measles). Major epidemics had been occurring in 7-year cycles (in 1967, 1974, 1981). In 1982-3, all girls aged 12 - 14 are vaccinated in school; then all 12-year-old girls until 1986. By 1986, all girls aged 12-17 (more than a half million) have been vaccinated.

1984-5: An anti-tetanus vaccination campaign for the elderly is initiated. 3rd- and 4th- year medical students in a work-study program immunize 200,000 people over the age of 60.

1985: Tetanus boosters are given to the housewives vaccinated in 1975, and to the elderly.

1986: Vaccination of all population under age 15 for tetanus/diphtheria/whooping cough, measles, German measles, and mumps, reaching 2 million youth (96% coverage).

1988-90: All Cubans under age 20 are vaccinated for meningococcal meningitis B — a Cuban vaccine unique in the world.

<u>1990s:</u>

1990: Testing begins for the development of a recombinant vaccine against hepatitis B.

1991 : The vaccine for meningococcal meningitis B is included in the national vaccination program.

1992: The hepatitis B vaccine is also included in the national vaccination program; more than 3 million Cubans are immunized. Currently the whole Cuban population under the age of 18, as well as those in high risk groups of other ages, is protected.

1997: Cuba begins human trials of an AIDS vaccine — a year before the United States.

1999: All babies born since 1998 are vaccinated against hemophilous influenza. Research continues on AIDs and cancer vaccines.

How Has So Much Innovative Work Been Possible In A Small, Blockaded, Island Nation?

Cuba's government has made huge investments in this area, both in capital and in human resources, even in the years of greatest economic difficulty. Cuba's biotechnology institutes use a sophisticated model which is based on collaboration instead of competition, and which is fully integrated with the health care service system. Cuban biotechnology is not market-driven; it's driven by health needs.

~When ex-President Carter visited Cuba in May 2002, he asked a Cuban scientist, "Could Cuban vaccines help children in the US?"

Dr. Concepcion Campa, Director of the Carlos J.

Finlay institute, and inventor of the meningitis B vaccine, replied - "That would be our greatest desire!"~

Cuba's Fight Against Aids

Human trials are currently under way for a Cuban AIDS vaccine. (The young scientists who worked on developing the vaccine had so much confidence in their work that they volunteered to be subjects in the clinical trials — to be injected with the HIV virus as well as the vaccine.) Treatment of HIV/AIDS in Cuba has included comprehensive universal testing and establishment of special sanatoriums. Although there were some complaints that patients' personal freedoms were restricted, the spread of the virus was quickly controlled, and people with AIDS were guaranteed access to high-protein meals and a low-stress environment (this at the height of the "special period," when food was in profoundly short supply and medications such as AZT were almost completely unavailable because of the US blockade). The low frequency of HIV/AIDS in Cuba reflects the benefits of these treatment approaches. In 1997, 1100 Cubans in a population of 11 million were HIV+ — a frequency rate of 1/10,000. By 2000, due in part to increases in tourism, approximately 1000 more Cubans were infected with the virus, bringing the frequency to 1/5,000. Compare this with the US frequency rate, which is close to 1/300 or the rates in sub-Saharan Africa, which approach 1/25.

Health Care Is A Right

Cuban health statistics reflect the Cubans' commitment to health care as a basic human right. Cuba considers that it's the government's responsibility to satisfy the needs and increase the well-being of families, citizens, and society. It continues to emphasize the needs of the most vulnerable population groups: children, women, and the elderly.

The Cuban health system is considered to be "a necessity for the very health of the revolution." Even with their successes and their extraordinary health indicators, they are not resting on their laurels, but are working on improving services, renovating facilities, and raising the level of patient care. Even in the depths of a profound economic crisis, they have not cut back on services; they have not closed a single hospital or clinic.

Contrast this with health care management elsewhere in the world. Currently the US is intentionally training *fewer* doctors; hospitals are being merged, privatized, and sometimes shut down; HMOs and insurance restrictions limit patient care. Developing nations are told they can't get foreign aid or credit from world banks unless they cut their spending on health care and other social services. Cuba has refused to adopt this model, and has worked to keep its system running "without having to apply the neoliberal formulas imposed by the greatest world power."

>> "Cuba's health indicators are comparable to those of the world's richest nations. What this means is that you can get significant health performance without being rich - if you use your resources wisely." ~ Dr. Luis Herrera, Director, *Cuban Center for Biotechnology and Genetic Engineering*

The US Blockade Attacks Cuba's Health Care System

Since 1962, the US economic blockade of Cuba has prohibited the acquisition of pharmaceutical products, medical equipment and supplies from US sources. For many years, Cuba compensated for the loss of US products by trading heavily with the Soviet bloc. But with the collapse of the Soviet Union in 1991, Cuba lost its secure markets for nearly 85% of its imports, including 63% of its food, 98% of its fuel, 80% of its raw materials, and 80% of its equipment and machinery.

At that point, the US could have declared an end to its Cold War policy and eased its restrictions against Cuba. Instead, prompted by powerful and wealthy far-right-wing Cuban- American interest groups, the US decided to make its blockade even stronger. In exchange for campaign money from their right-wing supporters, Torricelli, Helms and Burton led the charge in the Congress to make the US blockade even more punishing to Cuba.

The Torricelli Law (1992)

>> Banned foreign subsidiaries of US corporations from trading with Cuba.

>> Banned ships which stop in Cuba from docking in US ports for 180 days.

>> Restricted Cuba's access to international financing and credit.

With this law, all pharmaceutical products manufactured by international subsidiaries of US drug companies became completely unavailable for purchase in Cuba. Under this law, foreign corporations which are partially owned by US corporations are barred from selling medicines and medical equipment to Cuba. Numerous foreign firms which had traditionally sold medical equipment or spare parts to Cuba broke their commercial ties when the US Treasury Department turned down their requests for export licenses because they were partially owned by a US corporation. Freight costs for medical shipments skyrocketed, because any company shipping to Cuba had to forego stopping at a US port or else risk confiscation of their ship. And as US conglomerates continued to swallow up foreign manufacturers through mergers and acquisitions, more and more medications — 50% of the most commonly used worldclass" drugs — became off-limits to Cuba.

The Helms/Burton Law (1996)

>> Added further restrictions on trade with Cuba.

>> Added further pressure on other nations to restrict their trade with Cuba.

Since 1991, when the fall of the Soviet bloc triggered the economic crisis which the Cubans call the "special period in peacetime," these two US laws have served not only to maintain the US blockade of Cuba but also to progressively strengthen it. Cuba's economic losses have affected all sectors of the economy, have directly or indirectly affected all aspects of the health care system, and have threatened the lives of Cuba's most vulnerable: the children, the elderly, and the infirm.

"We Have Not Been Able To Buy A Single Aspirin"

Medicines, chemicals and raw materials for the pharmaceutical industry, disposable medical supplies, new medical equipment, and spare parts for medical and nonmedical technical equipment have all been in critically short supply in Cuba since the passage of the Torricelli Law. More than half of the most commonly used world-class drugs are manufactured by US corporations or their subsidiaries, and therefore are essentially unavailable in Cuba unless they happen to arrive in small unpredictable quantities in a shipment of donations. As US businesses continue their corporate takeovers of other medical industries around the world, the effects of the Torricelli Law only get worse for Cuba. Here are two examples:

>> Cuba used to purchase pacemakers for cardiac patients from a division of the Siemens Corporation based in Sweden. When the pacemaker division of Siemens was purchased by the St. Jude Hospital Corporation in St. Paul, Minnesota, those pacemakers became unavailable to Cuba.

>> When Editorial Interamericana was acquired by the US publishing house McGraw Hill, the new US parent corporation pressured its new acquisition to stop selling medical textbooks to Cuba — even though it's not illegal to sell books and informational materials to Cuba.

The Blockade And The "Special Period"

In 1997, the American Association for World Health (AAWH), which serves as the US committee for the World Health Organization (WHO) and the Pan American Health Organization (PAHO), published a 300-page report on how the US embargo has affected health care and nutrition in Cuba. We have also been eyewitnesses to these negative effects, in repeated trips to Cuba during the years of the "special period": Many common medicines manufactured by US firms or their subsidiaries —antibiotics, cancer medicines, asthma medicines, aspirins — have been virtually unavailable in Cuba.

>> An epidemic of optic neuropathy, linked to food shortages, blinded 50,000 Cuban adults in 1992-3.

>> Children on the cancer ward of the Juan Manuel Marquez Pediatric Hospital in Marianao were vomiting 28-30 times a day, for lack of a US-made anti-nausea medicine used to control the side effects of chemotherapy.

>> A lack of spare parts disabled countless pieces of essential hospital equipment.

>> Surgeries dropped from 885,790 in 1990 to 536,547 in 1995 — a glaring indicator of the decline in hospital resources such as anesthetics, catheters, sutures, instruments, disposable supplies, antibiotics, cyclosporin and other necessary medicines.

>> Malnutrition among pregnant women led to the first increase in low birth-weight babies since 1959. (Licensing restrictions, shipping penalties, and pressure on US trading partners restricted Cuba's access not only to food but also to fertilizers and animal feed for food production.)

>> Water-borne bacterial infections, such as giardia, increased as water quality deteriorated for lack of US-made spare parts and purification chemicals.

>> A lack of machine parts and special low-radiation X-ray film curtailed Cuba's award winning mobile

mammography program for early detection of breast cancer.

>> AIDS patients had to wait as long as six months for AZT, if it was available at all. Cuba lost markets for selling its own medicines and vaccines, and lost access to international sources of medical information.

The US Government Denies The Deadly Nature Of Its Cuba Policies

The US government continues to try to put a pretty face on its brutal blockade policy— and to some extent they have been successful until recently, because the travel blockade and the information blockade against Cuba have prevented most US citizens from seeing the real effects of US policy. The US continues to insist that "we send *lots* of aid to Cuba," and then they grant a few licenses for token amounts of aid, to try to prove their point. (They even inflate their aid totals by including the unlicensed aid which has been delivered to Cuba by IFCO's Pastors for Peace caravans — even though they've done everything in their power to try to stop that aid from being delivered!) But a health care system as sophisticated as Cuba's, serving 11.5 million people, cannot be run on the basis of small random shipments of donated medicines.

The US government also claims that any US corporation that wants to can get a Treasury or Commerce license to sell medicines to Cuba. But in reality, the licensing requirements are so prohibitive that US pharmaceutical companies have practically given up trying to sell to the Cuban market until the blockade is ended. US licensing requirements include "end-use monitoring," which means that a company that sells to Cuba has to vouch for what happened to every aspirin they sold. This creates a bureaucratic nightmare for the selling corporation, and compromises the buyer's ability to provide quality care. Dr. Anthony Kirkpatrick, a Florida physician, used a Freedom of Information Act request to study all US Commerce licenses for medical sales to Cuba. He found that less than $1.6 million worth of medicines and medical equipment had actually been sold to Cuba by the US since the Torricelli Law went into effect in 1992 (Kirkpatrick later lost his federal job for "whistle-blowing"; the Government Accountability Project is working with him on his appeal.)

Support for a more humane US policy toward Cuba has been growing. In the last few years, a strong majority of the US Congress has voted repeatedly to lift restrictions on sales of food and medicine to Cuba. But manoeuvres by the House Republican leadership and Cuban-American members of Congress have prevented these bills and amendments from taking effect as they were intended. A bill was passed in 2001 to allow the sale of food and medicine to Cuba. But in absence of provisions for credit, financing, shipping and insurance; with restrictive US licensing regulations still in place; and with the exorbitant prices of US pharmaceuticals, trade is still severely limited. The US administration and the right-wing Cuban-American lobby have difficulty defending the brutality of the policy, and so they lie about it. They claim that the US sends lots of aid to Cuba. But more and more US citizens are seeing through these lies, and are asking our government to stop using medicine as a weapon in our undeclared war against Cuba.

Ingenuity And Resourcefulness: "We're Better Doctors Now"

One of the most profound indicators of the outstanding quality of Cuba's medical professionals has been the grace-under-pressure with which they have responded to the acute economic crisis brought on by the US blockade. When medicines disappeared from the pharmacy shelves, or when broken-down machines could not be fixed, the Cuban professionals kept working, trying to devise new solutions to increase preventive care, to develop new medicines, to share limited resources.

For example:

>> A family doctor's shelves might be bare - but in the yard behind the office s/he will show you the orange tree, and how they've boiled the leaves to make cough syrup, and used the bark for poultices for wounds.

>> We visited a hospital whose parking lot was no

longer being used because of fuel shortages. Everyone who came to the hospital was on bicycle or on horseback. The asphalt on the lot had been torn up, and hospital staff were using the lot to grow aloe plants to make burn ointments, skin creams, and other medicines.

>> "Because things don't come easily to us, we have had to think harder, to rely on each other more, to become more resourceful, and to find new solutions to better serve our patients."- *a Cuban family doctor*

>> During the worst days of the "special period," doctors' offices operated, often for months at a time, without soap, without disinfectants, without spare sheets and towels. If equipment broke down, it stayed broken, since spare parts were unavailable. In one clinic we visited, the nurse explained that the neighbours who are the clinic's patients had brought in spare *paper* from their own houses: otherwise there would have been no paper to keep the clinic's medical records.

Despite Hardships, Health Care Remains Cuba's Priority

Cuba has continues to prioritize its public health services, and this is reflected in Cuba's national budget allocations for health care. In 1990, health care accounted for 6.6% of the Cuban national budget; in 1997 it was 10.9%. Expenditures on health care per inhabitant actually increased 27% from 1990 to 1997 — in spite of the extreme shortage of hard currency which affected every aspect of Cuba's economy in those years. In 1994, the availability of hard currency for the health sector was only 39.6% of what it had been in 1989, but by 1997 it was up again to 49.4% - still only half what it had been before the special period, but with significant improvement over three years.

Since 1993, virtually all of the hard currency budgeted to the Cuban Health Ministry has been used to import medicines, raw materials, and disposable supplies; all other expenditures have had to take place through subsidized trade or in Cuban pesos. This constriction of available hard currency and trade options has reduced Cuba's capacity to acquire medical supplies from low-priced foreign markets to only 20-30% of what it was before the fall of the Soviet bloc.

Cuba has been grateful for whatever donations have come from foreign governments, non-governmental organizations, solidarity groups, and friends of Cuba around the world. But a national health care system for 11.5 million people cannot function on donations alone. Cuban doctors who need specialized medicines to treat critically ill patients should not have to depend on whatever medicines might happen to arrive in a particular box of donations. Cuba has begun to find new ways to generate income to maintain its health care services. Much of the income from Cuba's growing tourism industry is dedicated to the public health budget. (As a hotel manager explained to us, "Our profits don't go into the pocket of a Donald Trump; they go to pay for medical care.") The recent development of "health tourism" in Cuba includes not just plastic surgery or special treatments, but also anti-stress institutes which offer acupuncture, sulfur springs, mud baths and massage.

Cubans like to say: "we live like poor people but we die like rich people." And disease control efforts continue to improve; the frequency of infectious and parasitic diseases in children ages 0-4 decreased by more than half in 1988-1997, a period which included Cuba's worst economic crisis. The Cuban people have found ways to chip in and help. Workers who have access to dollars (hotel and restaurant workers who receive tips, for example) have been asked to make voluntary contributions from their tip money to help support the national health care system. In 1997 these workers contributed a total of $1,800,000 toward national health care — funds which were used for the development of maternal/child care, cancer, and kidney programs. And members of the block committees — Committees for the Defense of the Revolution — make a half million blood donations every year.

INTERNATIONALISM: A PROUD TRADITION OF CUBAN HEALTH CARE

Cuba's first international health brigade went to Algeria in 1963, and Cuba has been proud to say that one of its leading exports has been doctors and health care professionals. Cuban health care brigades have served in all parts of Africa and Latin America.

>> Currently there are more than 600 Cuban doctors giving needed services in the most under-served townships of South Africa, and Cuba has set up medical schools — with Cuban professors — in South Africa to train new Black South African doctors who were not able to study under apartheid.

>> When Cuban diplomats in Moscow became aware that the Soviet government was covering up the devastating effects of the Chernobyl nuclear disaster, the Cuban government made an immediate response.

They opened a long-term treatment facility on the seacoast at Tarará, where 18,000 children of Chernobyl have received long-term treatment for radiation sickness, thyroid cancer, leukemia, skin disorders, and post-traumatic stress — all free of charge.

>> In 1998, when Hurricanes Mitch and Georges devastated parts of Central America and the Caribbean, Cuba immediately established a serious program to meet the health care needs of the afflicted nations. The idea of Cuba's Comprehensive Health Care Program for the Nations Affected by Hurricane Mitch was to save as many lives each year as were lost in Hurricane Mitch — 30,000 lives each year, including as many as 25,000 children and youth — simply by expanding basic health care, reducing infant mortality, and controlling curable diseases.

>> Cuba sent 2000 doctors and health care workers — free of charge and for as long as necessary — to provide desperately needed health services in the hardest hit and most remote areas. (In 1999, one of IFCO's Pastors for Peace caravans visited the remains of the Nicaraguan village of Posoltega.) Hundreds of lives were lost there when a mudslide raged down the deforested mountainside where residents had built their tiny homes. Months after the hurricane, 5,000 survivors of the mudslide were still living huddled under plastic tarps. They were receiving only limited help from the Nicaraguan government. The Nicaraguan doctors were reluctant to go to the most remote,

disease-ridden regions — but Cuban doctors had set up a clinic, right there in the hardest-hit area, and we saw them working around the clock to provide basic medical care to this devastated community.

>> Cuba opened a new medical school to train Central American physicians. The initial offer of 500 full scholarships each year means that in the next 10 years, Cuba will train more than 5000 new doctors for Central America and the Caribbean. This remarkable program, the Latin American School of Medicine, has grown rapidly to include 10,000 students from 30 nations in the Americas and Africa.

>> Even students from the United States -- from communities of color and low-income communities — have been invited to receive full scholarships for medical training at the Latin American Medical School. This generous offer includes tuition, room and board, books, uniforms, and a small stipend for six years of medical study. The scholarship offer comes as Cuba's response to the so-called 'third world' conditions which exist in many urban and rural regions of the richest nation in the world, and the urgent need for more accessible health care in our nation's most disenfranchised communities. Cuba's scholarship offer comes with only one condition: that students return home to the US after they graduate from medical school, to give service in our own nation's most underserved communities.

>> The first US students to enroll in the Latin American Medical School entered in 2001; 117 US students are enrolled in the spring 2009 semester, and new students will be admitted each year in September and March. The program is internationally accredited, and students are receiving preparation for US licensing exams.

[If you are interested in promoting or participating in this remarkable scholarship program, please contact IFCO for more information:

418 West 145th Street,
NYC 10031;
212/926-5757; ifco@igc.org.]

Cuban medicines, vaccines, and biotechnology have also benefited developing countries around the world. Organic pesticides developed in Cuba's LABIOFAM laboratories, which are specially designed to destroy rodents without harming the environment, were used to control an epidemic of rats in Managua, Nicaragua in 1997. Hundreds of thousands of doses of Cuba's meningitis B vaccine were donated to Uruguay to control an epidemic which was killing Uruguayan children. Cuba's international health services are based on a simple and prophetic vision: that it is possible to address the systemic health care needs of chronically underdeveloped nations. Cuba knows that it's possible to lower high infant mortality rates and to raise low life expectancies. Cuba knows that children need not die of curable diseases, for lack of simple medicines and the doctors to administer them. Cuba knows from its own experience, because Cuba has achieved extraordinary health indicators for its own people — even under the conditions of a cruel US economic blockade.

STRIVING FOR PERFECTION: NEW DEVELOPMENTS IN CUBAN HEALTH CARE

In 1998 the Cuban Ministry of Health announced a five-year plan to renovate and improve health care services in Cuba — to repair facilities which have suffered physical deterioration, to improve management training, to achieve even better health indicators, and to raise the people's level of satisfaction with their health care. Rather than cut back on services, or close clinics and hospitals, or privatize, or limit coverage, Cuba continues to focus on improving coverage, accessibility, equity and quality of care. Some current programs and strategies:

>> A national program of natural and traditional medicines. Acute shortages of world-class pharmaceuticals, due to the US economic blockade, have encouraged Cuba to explore and develop holistic and

non-western methods of health care. Cuba has been developing its capacity to produce 80% of the 900 items used in the Cuban medical dispensary — and by producing these medicines locally, they expect to save 4-5 times the current cost of importing these medicines. Cuban laboratory scientists are currently working hard on developing 91 essential drugs and vaccines on which people's lives depend, and an additional 349 prescription medicines which make up the nation's Basic Chart of Medicines. Their priority is to identify and try to self-produce all the medicines that the population currently needs. Cuban doctors are also expanding their use of natural medicines and treatment modalities such as acupuncture, acupressure, laser therapy, medicinal baths, and homeopathy. Their goal is not only to compensate for shortages of US medicines, but also to develop a new Cuban model of natural holistic medicine which can be used in Cuba and in developing nations — which then can achieve improved health and self-sufficiency, and become less dependent on the world market.

>> Revitalization of the hospitals.

Cuba's economic crisis and the US blockade have affected Cuba's capacity to offer surgery and emergency services. Cuba's hospitals need physical renovation, new equipment, spare parts, and all sorts of basic supplies.

>> Revitalization of research and technology.

Resources are being sought to expand the work of Cuba's special institutes to study of cancer, kidney and heart disease, and congenital defects.

>> Improvements in dental and optical services and emergency care

Dental and optical services have suffered from the lack of resources. Materials and medical equipment to make fillings, dental bridges, and eye-glasses have been extremely scarce since 1992. [A Cuban Health Ministry report points out that nearly 20% of Cuba's population needs eyeglasses —one of the results of having such a highly literate population!!]

>> Focus on control of transmittable and non-transmittable diseases

Cuba continues to expand its programs of universal vaccination, early diagnosis, and biotechnology to control contagious diseases. But more than 2/3 of the mortality rate in Cuba comes from non-transmittable diseases —heart attacks, cancer, cardiovascular diseases, and accidents. Cuba's family doctors and nurses continue to promote and develop new programs to improve nutrition and deal with the health risks which are associated with lifestyle, such as obesity, sedentary lifestyle, smoking, and inadequate diet.

>> Maternal/child health

Cuba's comprehensive program continues to focus on improving the reproductive health of women and their partners; decreasing the incidence of low birth weight, prenatal infections, and acute respiratory infections; and improving early diagnosis of cervical/uterine cancers. In this area as in others, natural methods are strongly promoted. Breastfeeding is encouraged; and the innovative and holistic "Skin to Skin" program focuses on increasing physical contact between mothers and their premature infants, which helps the babies to thrive.

>> Attention to the older adult

With demographic shifts brought about by improved life expectancy statistics, the number of elderly in the Cuban population is increasing. In 1997, 12.9% of Cuba's population was over age 60; in the year 2000, 14% were over 60; in 2025 it will be 21%. Cuba plans to continue to focus on meeting the bio-psychosocial needs of the elderly, emphasizing primary care, community support and non-institutional alternatives to improve quality of life for Cuba's elderly.

An Inspiration to the World

We who live in the US have much to learn from Cuba's model of health care which is universal, free of charge, and accessible to all. And, as US citizens, we have a responsibility to be better informed about the effects of US policies, such as the US blockade of Cuba, on our neighbour nations. As eyewitnesses to Cuba's health care system, we have been impressed with Cuba's consistent emphasis on providing care for "the least of these" — in Cuba as well as in some of the world's most poor and desperate nations. The unfailing dedication of Cuban health care professionals has led to dramatic improvements in quality of life, for millions of people who

previously had no other hope of receiving decent medical care. IFCO/Pastors for Peace is pleased to honour the diligent health care professionals of the Cuban health care system. We especially pay tribute to Cuba's national leadership, whose vision of universal health care as a right of every citizen sets an example for the world.

Nations Where Cuba Offered Health Assistance in 2002

AMERICAS
Antigua & Barbuda
Argentina
Aruba
Bahamas
Belize
Bolivia
Brazil
Chile
Colombia
Costa Rica
Dominica
Dominican Republic
Dutch Antilles Bonaire
Ecuador
El Salvador
Guatemala
Guyana
Grenada
Haiti
Honduras

Jamaica
Mexico
Panama
Paraguay
Peru
St Lucia
St Kitts & Nevis
St. Vincent & the Grenadines
Surinam
Trinidad & Tobago
United States of America
Venezuela

ASIA
Bhutan
Cambodia
Laos
Maldives
Sri Lanka

CENTRAL AND EASTERN EUROPE:
Italy
Portugal
Spain
Switzerland
Ukraine

AFRICA
Angola

Botswana
Burkina Faso
Cape Verde
Equatorial Guinea
Ethiopia
Gambia
Ghana
Guinea
Guinea Bissau
Mali
Mozambique
Namibia
Niger
Nigeria
Sahel Republic
Yemen
Sao Tome & Principe
Seychelles
South Africa
Uganda
Zambia
Zimbabwe

What Can You Do?

If reading this pamphlet has inspired you to want to give support to the achievements of the Cuban health care system, you can:

>> Join an IFCO/Pastors for Peace Friendshipment

Caravan to Cuba, as a means of challenging the US government ban on travel and the sending of unlicensed humanitarian aid to Cuba.

>> Support the caravans by providing medical aid, or the financing to send aid.

>> Help recruit US students to the Latin American School of Medicine by publicizing this scholarship program in your community. Brochures and application forms are available from IFCO: 212/926-5757.

>> Lobby your senators and Congressional representatives to persuade them to support legislation aimed at lifting the blockade.

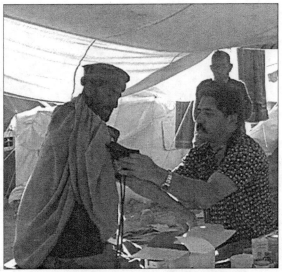
Cuban doctor working in Khanpur, Pakistan, 2005.

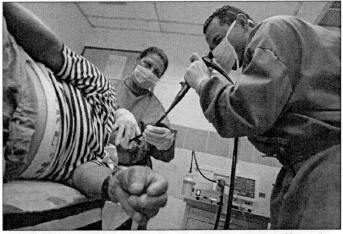
Cuban doctors working in the Barrio Adentro social mission in Venezuela, 2006.

Cuban medical volunteers prepare to go to New Orleans following Hurricane Katrina, 2005. The US government declined the offer of assistance.

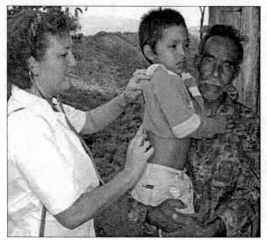

A Cuban doctor volunteers in a rural community in Venezuela, 2006.

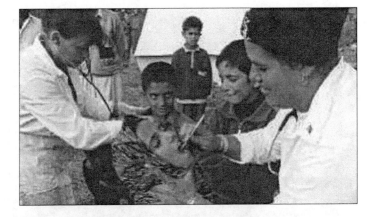

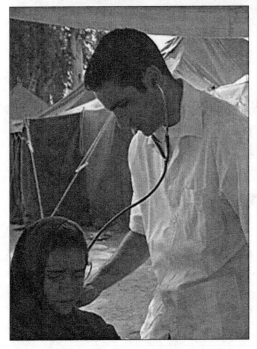

Above: Cuban
doctors working in
Bat Sanghra village,
Pakistan, 2005.

Left: Cuban doctor
checks on a patient
in Khanpur, Pakistan,
December 2005.

International students at the Latin American School of Medicine in Havana, Cuba, December 2006.

U.S. graduates of the Latin American School of Medicine, 2007.

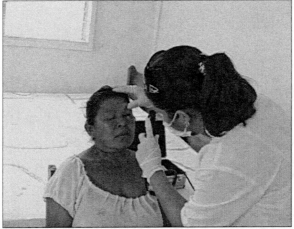

Cuban doctor treats a woman from an Indigenous community in
Paramakatoi, Guyana, 2009.

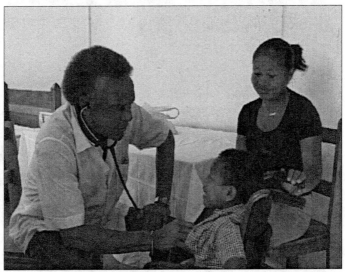

Cuban doctor treats a child from an Indigenous community in
Paramakatoi, Guyana, 2009.

Cuban doctors volunteering in Zanzibar, Tanzania, 2009.

Cuban medical students march in a rally in Havana.

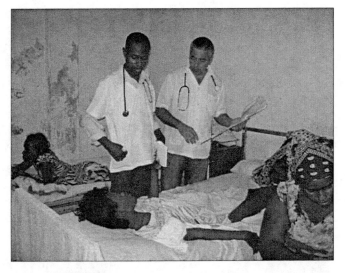

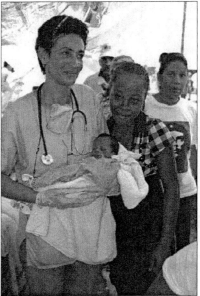

Above: Cuban and Haitian doctors treat earthquake victims in Haiti, January 2010.

Left: Cuban doctor assisting with childbirth in earthquake-stricken Haiti, January 2010.

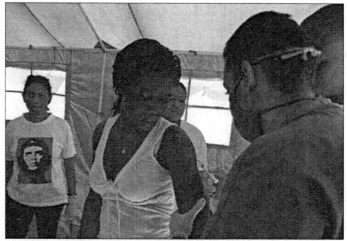

Cuban doctors treat victims of an earthquake in Haiti, January 2010.

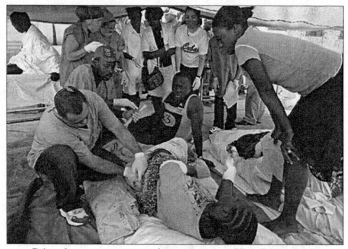

Cuban doctors treat victims of an earthquake in Haiti, January 2010.

U.S. graduates of Cuba's Latin American School of Medicine volunteer with the Cuban medical brigade in Haiti following the 2010 earthquake.

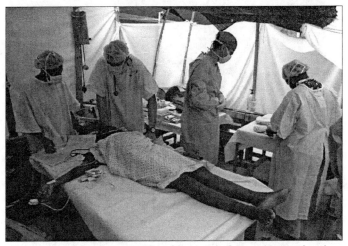

Cuban doctors assist patient in Haiti following the January 2010 earthquake.

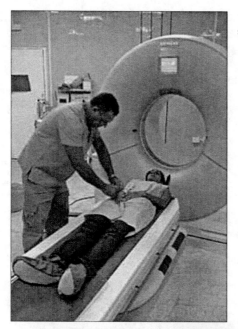

Left: Doctor administers a CT scan to a patient in a clinic in Cuba.

Below: Doctor evaluates a patient in a Cuban clinic.

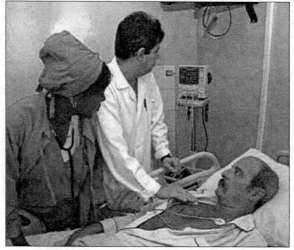

Cuban doctors assist patient in Haiti following the January 2010 earthquake.

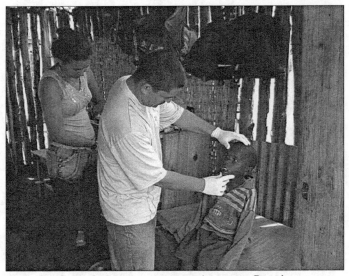

Cuban doctors on an international mission in Rwanda.

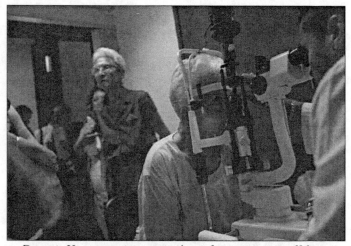

Doctor in Havana examines a patient's eyes for surgery as part of Mision Milagro, a project to restore the eyesight of millions in Latin America for free.

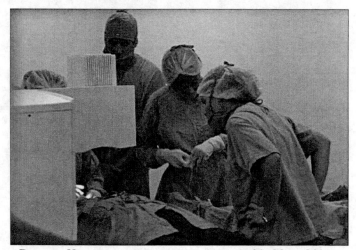

Doctors in Havana carry out eye surgery on a patient of the Mision Milagro project.

Left: at a maternity home for pregnant women in Vinales, Cuba.

Below: a Cuban man gets a checkup from the dentist.

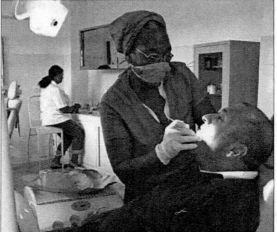

Above and below: a Cuban doctor volunteering with the Cuban medical team
in Pakistan after an earthquake.

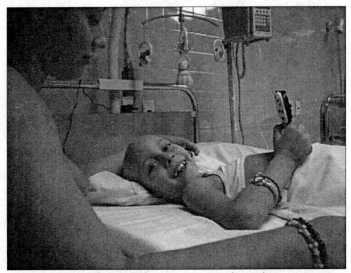

A Cuban child gets treatment in a hospital.

Cuban medical students march in a commemoration of eight medical students killed in the fight against Spanish colonialism in Cuba.

"12 hours of the blockade is equivilant to all the insulin needed annually for the 64 thousand patients of the country." Havana, Cuba, 2010

"For the World" Sancti Spiritus Province, Cuba, 2010

"The most precious of our medicine is human capital." Havana, Cuba, 2000.

APPENDIX

Speech by Fidel Castro to the First Graduating Class of the Latin American School of Medicine

Speech given by Dr Fidel Castro Ruz, President of the Republic of Cuba, at the first graduation of students from the Latin American School of Medicine. Karl Marx Theatre, August 20, 2005.

Excellencies and dear friends who, in representation of the countries that are home to the doctors who graduate here today, honour us with your presence;

Tenacious and dedicated young people who graduate today as a new class doctor, and their families;

Professors and workers of the Latin American School of Medicine;

Dear compatriots from Cuba, the Caribbean and Latin America;

Distinguished guests:

Almost seven years ago this graduation ceremony was merely a dream. Today, it is a confirmation of the power of human beings to reach the loftiest of goals, and it is truly a prize for those of us who believe that a better world lies within our grasp.

The idea was born when the news services began to report that Hurricane Mitch had taken the lives of more than 40,000 people in Central America. We proposed to send a medical corps that would save, on a yearly basis, as many lives as those, which had been taken by the hurricane. We did not hesitate to do this, even though we were still enduring the worst of the Special Period. It was made possible because, even in the midst of those terrible tribulations that followed the collapse of the socialist block and the USSR, which deprived us from all outside cooperation, and at a time when the world had given up our cause for lost, the Revolution never ceased, for one moment, creating human capital.

Together with the idea of helping Central America by sending over thousands of doctors, the Latin American School of Medicine sprang into being, with the aim of progressively replacing the Cuban medical personnel with local doctors, as the former completed their missions. Today this school, with its ever-expanding development, helps to train doctors not only in Central America, but also in other parts of the world.

Looking back in retrospect, we remember that before January 1, 1959, a bloody and repressive regime closed down hundreds of our institutions of higher education, including the only Medical School at the University of Havana.

Most of the graduates came from economically secure families. Half of the doctors, lured by the United States, abandoned their threatened and assaulted Homeland. Only three thousand doctors and a reduced number of Professors of Medicine stayed. Alongside them we began to build what we have today.

Because of this, only a handful of students graduated as doctors during the first years following the triumph of the Revolution. The first graduation of young doctors who had begun their studies after January 1, 1959 took place on November 14, 1965.

Our armed struggle in the eastern range of the Sierra Maestra had ended hardly six years earlier. With memories of that conflict fresh in my mind, I invited that group of 400 young people who were completing their medical studies to hold the graduation ceremony on the highest peak in that range and in Cuba, at an altitude of two thousand meters, that is, at the Turquino Peak.

Today, as I stand before you in this theatre, the words that I spoke to those graduating doctors on the summit of that steep mountain seem unreal.

After underlining some paragraphs from that speech,

I cannot resist the temptation to repeat some of the things that I said then tonight, when a group of 1,610 doctors are graduating from the Latin American School of Medicine, including graduates from the Caribbean who studied in other Cuban universities.

At that time, we were also victims of constant pirate attacks and acts of terrorism directed against our country, which were organized by the government of the United States.

This is what I said to those young people at the time: "In this journey, many of you had the opportunity to understand many things, things unspoken, without indoctrination, without speeches, transmitted in this soundless but highly eloquent language that speaks of social and human realities. I am sure that rather than abstract ideas, inclinations, vocation, and the natural condition of each and every one of you – which are unquestionably good – the factor that will make you live up to your duties and always act the best way possible, will be the attitude of the peasants of these mountains, the type of men and women that you have seen here; the goodness, friendliness, generosity, solidarity, appreciation, and gratitude of men, women, children and elderly people who have worked, grown and lived under such difficult conditions in these mountains; their truly spontaneous gestures, the flowers with which they welcomed you, the fruits of their harvests, the coffee, the water, their willingness to help you, their cooperation in all types of organization, their high regard for doctors."

"The oath taken by these graduating students, its internationalist and revolutionary spirit... all of this must be very painful to the enemy.

"Perhaps they tried to minimize this in some way, so last night, according to the news we received this morning at approximately 12:45 a.m., a pirate boat opened fire on the coast, in the area of Lagunas Street in Havana. Three or four minutes later, another pirate boat, apparently searching for the President's residence, opened fire and caused great damage with machine gun fire on the National Aquarium building. This happened just today."

I will try to make a brief summary of the results of our efforts with regard to the training of personnel and the development of medical sciences all along these years for the distinguished guests who honour us with their presence as well as for all those who are also present here at this graduation ceremony.

Medical doctors who graduated in our country following the triumph of the Revolution:

During the decade 1960-69: 4,907

During the second decade, 1970-79: 9,410

During the third decade, 1980-89: 22,490

During the fourth decade, 1990-99: 37,841

During the fifth decade, 2000-04: 9,334

The total reaches 83,982. Three thousand six hundred and twelve out of this big total have come from other countries. We must also add the 1,905 Cuban doctors graduating this year, which means that the total actually reaches 85,887.

Nowadays the methods used to train doctors are radically different. Before the Revolution, the size of school classes was huge, practical lessons were minimal, and the fundamentals of basic sciences were virtually non-existent. Students were able to graduate without having ever directly examined a patient or assisted a childbirth. The curriculum was mainly aimed at curing patients and the private practice of the profession. These features were far removed from the health problems, thus affecting the country. The word prevention was hardly ever used. On average, 300 doctors and 30 dentists graduated each year.

Today the number of youth from Cuba and from other countries around the world, who are ever more united in the struggle for a more just and humane future, is rising considerably in the different areas required by a logical and efficient public health system.

During the academic year 2004-2005, the students' breakdown was as follows:

Medicine: 28,071

Dentistry: 2,758

Nursing: 19,530

Health Technology: 28,400

Current students' sum total: 78,759

Currently, more than 12,000 medical students from 83 different countries are studying for their degree in our country:

5,500 come from South American countries

3,244 come from Central American countries

489 come from Mexico and North America, including 65 young people coming from the United States and two from Puerto Rico.

1,039 come from the Caribbean

777 come from Sub-Saharan Africa

42 come from 6 countries in Northern Africa and the Middle East

61 come from Asia

2 come from Europe

The Latin American countries with the largest numbers of students in Cuba are:

Venezuela 889

Honduras 711

Guatemala 701

Paraguay 641

Brazil 629

Bolivia 567

Nicaragua 560

Ecuador 551

Colombia 545

Peru 532

From the Caribbean:

Haiti 676

The Dominican Republic 403

Jamaica 134

Guyana 117

Belize 79

Saint Lucia 69

Today we have the enormous satisfaction of seeing you, 1,610 new doctors, graduate:

495 from South America

771 from Central America

343 from the Caribbean

1 from the U.S.A.

Over the past seven years our battle for solidarity and

for the training of doctors from Cuba and from other sister nations has been intense and ever-increasing.

The means and the methodology have been incredibly revolutionized, and theoretical and practical training has considerably surpassed that which had traditionally prevailed throughout history. It would be more accurate to say that the traditional form of training has been improved several times over.

While in the past there was only one university hospital, now all hospitals fall into the honourable category of university hospitals.

What is more: today, any of the 444 polyclinics which offer primary medical care can also serve as medical training centers. With the support of audio visual aids and interactive computer software, plus the assistance of dozens of specialists, Master degree and even PhD's holders, our results can compare and are even superior to those achieved by past methods used to train those who must ensure the health and well-being of the people.

Seven months ago I had the great satisfaction of meeting with 300 young people from Haiti, Guatemala and Honduras, who were in the midst of their last semester of studies and were about to return to their respective countries to work alongside brigades of Cubans specialized in General Comprehensive Medicine, who were working in the most far-flung corners of this region. They were accompanied by 50 young Cubans from the same level of studies. The results have been impressive. I promised them that I would attend their graduation ceremony, and here they are, as part of this very crowd, standing shoulder to shoulder like Spartan soldiers of Medicine, brandishing their victorious shields.

Glory be to these young people! Glory be to these new saviours of lives who are taking this noble medical profession to new heights of dedication and ethics, never before seen in this world! They embody the kind of doctors claimed for with desperate urgency by billions of people.

However, everything that I have said so far pales in comparison to the colossal movement that is being promoted by Venezuela and Cuba to train doctors ready to march in the vanguard of the Bolivarian dawn. Thanks to this, and as part of the "Barrio Adentro" Mission developed by President Hugo Chavez, 22,043 Venezuelan under-graduates have now embarked on their pre-med studies in the 7,898 Barrio Adentro surgeries, in close cooperation with the Venezuelan Ministries of Higher Education and Public Health.

On October 3, they will begin their first-year studies in Medicine. In only ten years time, 40 thousand will be graduating.

Likewise, in Cuba we are developing a program to educate, in an equal length of time, 20 thousand Venezuelan doctors from the Ribas Mission and from high schools, as well as 30 thousand doctors from Latin American and Caribbean countries. These programs are available to young people from Latin American and the Caribbean who have not been able to study in the best high schools or been able to secure entry into medical schools due to their humble backgrounds.

Training a medical doctor in the United States will cost the family no less than 300,000 dollars. Cuba, however, is presently training more than

12,000 doctors for the Third World, thus contributing to the well being of these countries, to a value of more than three billion US dollars. If we train or help to train 100,000 doctors from other countries in a period of ten years, we will be contributing the equivalent of 30 billion U.S. dollars, despite the fact that Cuba is a small, Third World nation suffering from an economic blockade imposed by the United States.

What is the secret? It lies in the solid fact that the human capital is worth far more than the financial capital. Human capital involves not only knowledge, but also – and this is essential – conscience, ethics, solidarity, truly humane feelings, spirit of sacrifice, heroism, and the ability to make a little go a long way.

Rich countries do just what Cuba does, only the other way around. They don't train doctors for the Third World; they snatch the ones that are trained by these countries.

A report issued by the University of Harvard and the

World Health Organization denounces the scandalous plundering of doctors from poor countries by rich nations. A list was published with the total percentage of doctors from different countries who are Third World immigrants:

Austria 5 per cent

France 6 per cent

Germany 7 per cent

Denmark 7 per cent

Norway 15 per cent

Australia 22 per cent

United States 24 per cent

Canada 26 per cent

United Kingdom 32 per cent

New Zealand 35 per cent

The fact that these professionals leave their countries of origin means that, as the report points out, poor countries subsidize rich nations in this way with 500 million dollars every year.

These vast figures of which I speak are real and have their price in the capitalist market, but they do not require extensive material resources and can be, in fact, within the grasp of any country.

Venezuela and Cuba are cooperating together in one of the most exciting programs ever implemented: to return or preserve the sight of more than six million people in Latin America and the Caribbean.

Conditions have been created in Cuba, and are being developed in Venezuela, to diagnose, operate on or cure 25,000 people from the Caribbean, 100,000 from Cuba, 100,000 from Venezuela and 120,000 from South and Central America each year.

As a matter of fact, this program is already underway in 14 of the 24 ophthalmologic institutions that will become operational in our country by the end of this year. They have been equipped with the most advanced world-class technology available. Our country is now performing 1,500 eye surgeries per day.

This year we have reached the figure of 50,000 Venezuelans from the Barrio Adentro Mission who have undergone eye surgery as from the middle of January up until today, August 20. In less than a month 1,093 people from the Caribbean have received the same treatment, by virtue of the Agreements signed at the Venezuelan state of Anzontegui, on June 30 last.

It is important to note that every year, more than four and a half million people from Latin America and the Caribbean require this service, but do not receive it due to conditions of poverty, and more than half a million each year loose their sight, often without ever having been examined by a doctor.

Just as I did 40 years ago, please allow me to dream. The only difference being that now, after half a century of struggle, I am absolutely sure that no-one can say of our dreams what Calderon de la Barca once said: "...all life is a dream, and dreams themselves are only dreams."

Let us march forward! Forward, all of you invincible standard-bearers of such a noble profession, in demonstration of the fact that all the gold in the world cannot subdue the conscience of a true guardian of health and life, who is ready to go to any country where its services are required, convinced that a better world is possible!

Ever onwards to victory!

CUBA ANSWERS THE CALL FOR DOCTORS

Bulletin of the UN World Health Organization (WHO)
Volume 88, Number 5, May 2010

Havana's Latin American Medical School takes passionate young people from developing countries and sends them home as doctors. It's all about driving health equity, writes Gail Reed. Now the challenge is to get medical societies to accept them.

Dr Midalys Castilla is animated as she talks about the graduates of Havana's Latin American Medical School (ELAM) who are serving with Cuban medical teams in post-'quake Haiti. By the end of February, 557 of these ELAM graduates from 27 countries had made their way to Port-au-Prince, swelling the ranks of teams that will staff public health facilities past the emergency phase. "Doctors willing to go where they are most needed for as long as they are needed: this is the reason our school was established," says Castilla, academic vice-rector and a founder of the institution that was created after another disaster hit the region over a decade ago.

In 1998, hundreds of Cuban doctors were dispatched to the Dominican Republic, Guatemala, Haiti, Honduras and Nicaragua after two devastating hurricanes. Their services in remote, underserved communities begged the question of what would happen when they returned home.

This dilemma of sustainability prompted the decision to establish ELAM, its central campus located on Havana's western shoreline. The first students from Central America arrived in February 1999 and graduated from the six-year curriculum in 2005. Since then, 7248 physicians from 45 countries have obtained ELAM degrees, with current enrolment being 9362 students from 100 countries mainly in the Americas, the Middle East, Africa, Asia and the Pacific Islands.

In addition to its size, ELAM has other distinguishing features that align it with a handful of similar institutions worldwide founded expressly to address inequities in access to medical care. Medical schools in countries such as Australia, the Bolivarian Republic of Venezuela, Canada, the Philippines and South Africa share "social accountability" as their premise. The World Health Organization defines social accountability of medical schools as "the obligation to direct their education, research and service of activities towards addressing the priority health concerns of the community, region and/or nation that they have a mandate to serve".

ELAM's aim is to educate physicians primarily for public service in disadvantaged urban and rural communities, developing competencies in comprehensive primary care, from health promotion to treatment and rehabilitation. In exchange for a non-binding pledge to practise in underserved areas, students receive a full scholarship with a small monthly stipend, graduating debt-free.

Student recruitment processes for ELAM vary from country to country, where school administrators may involve representatives from Cuban embassies, local civil society, grassroots organizations or government in the selection process. Candidates must have at least a high-school diploma, a good academic record, aptitude and pass the admissions exam. Numbers of applicants can be daunting: third-year student Javier Montero from southern Chile recalls that more than 600 people applied for 60 places the year he was admitted to ELAM.

Preference is given to low-income applicants, who otherwise could not afford medical studies. "The result is that 75% of our student body comes from the kinds of communities that need doctors, including a broad representation of ethnic minorities and indigenous peoples," explains Castilla. For example, student Alfredo

Cayul's family is indigenous Mapuche and makes its living by subsistence farming in Chile; Jamaican Shereka Lewis's mother is a secretary, her stepfather a carpenter; Keitumetse Joyce Let'sela's widowed mother in Lesotho is a schoolteacher; and Vanessa Avila, from California, United States of America (USA), comes from a first-generation family of Mexican immigrants, her father being a gardener and her mother a housewife.

After enrolment, students spend three to six months in a pre-medical bridging programme to address uneven educational backgrounds. Non-Spanish speakers study the language, since instruction is in Spanish. The next two years focus on basic sciences, integrated in a new discipline called morphophysiology of the human body, including anatomy, physiology, embryology, histology and pathology. "This provides students with a more holistic understanding," says Castilla. These science studies are integrated with early clinical contact with patients, essentially at community clinics, with the aim of creating greater relevance to real-life clinical practice.

For the following three years, students are distributed among 14 medical universities across Cuba with some 32 000 Cuban medical students. There, clinical medicine – including patient relations – is melded with public health to build capacities for addressing health needs on a community as well as individual level.

These are the toughest years but also the most exciting, students say, because they are assigned patients under supervision as early as their third year. This is a significant departure from many curricula in Latin America, where even in the 1990s, a Pan American Health Organization study indicated that 70% of schools had no participation in their countries' health services and only 17% used primary care as an academic setting.

"We are learning medicine – I study at least five hours a day – and also about the human dimension of being a doctor from the example of our professors, and about the value of other health workers in the team," says third-year student Javier Montero of Chile, when asked what was most important to him about his clinical experience.

"We are bent on quality," says Ovidio Rodríguez, professor of internal medicine at the Salvador Allende General Teaching Hospital, where 168 ELAM students rotate through third year. "We aren't giving away grades. But we also work with students to help them succeed."

The fourth clinical year may be spent in Cuba or, in some cases, in the interns' home countries under the tutelage of Cuban medical professors. "This has the advantage of familiarizing interns with the health and social picture they will find when they graduate," says Juan Carrizo, ELAM's rector. "It also allows them to reconnect with their health system, communities and cultures."

Students who were interviewed commented on the bonds created by living and studying among peers from around the world. "The diversity that we thought would be our toughest problem has turned out to be our biggest strength," reflects Castilla. One delegate per country is elected to the Student Council, which also schedules activities dedicated to each nation's cultural heritage. Organizations such as the Student Movement of Native Peoples of the Americas (ME-POA) bring together the Aymara, Mapuche, Garifuna and other indigenous students, in what student leader Alfredo Cayul considers an important unifying experience.

During summer vacations, many students are involved in community service projects at home, "keeping us connected and aware", according to Pasha Jackson, a second-year student from Los Angeles, USA. A budding football star until sidelined by an injury, Pasha says memories of gang violence in his neighbourhood as well as his grandmother's nursing career made him want to "make a difference through medicine". He and 11 of the other 118 ELAM students from the USA spent last summer working with Native American tribal leaders and the University of New Mexico to understand conditions on the reservations and among the state's rural communities. "We need to see how we can apply what some consider an idealistic education to our own country now, learning how people live and the health disparities we will have to face."

His comments hint at the challenges confronted by innovative schools such as ELAM, which are struggling to be accepted by national medical societies and accreditation bodies. In the USA, 29 ELAM graduates are taking their licensing exams and another five have been accepted into residencies. The cost of taking such exams itself has been a problem for students in the USA and in other countries. But other graduates face bigger hurdles, as their degrees must be validated by sometimes reluctant medical societies and, even once they receive validation, there may be no jobs waiting for them in the public sector where they are most needed. "This is a big challenge," says Castilla. "But where the medical societies are more conscious of the need for these young physicians and where governments have committed resources to them, we are making progress."

The new doctors are at work in most countries in the Americas, including the USA, various African countries and much of the English-speaking Caribbean region.

ELAM, as well as the health systems around the world that incorporate its graduates, will ultimately be judged by its impact on the health status of the world's poorest. The need is indisputable: the average physician-to-population ratio in the 47 countries represented in ELAM's first graduating class of 1800 doctors was 0.98 physicians for every 1000 inhabitants, compared with Europe, which averages more than three per 1000 and Cuba at nearly six per 1000.

And at the same time, schools like ELAM present their own challenge to medical education across the globe to adopt a more socially committed agenda. As Charles Boelen, former coordinator of the World Health Organization's Human Resources for Health programme, comments: "This notion of social accountability (merits) attention worldwide, even within traditional medical circles ....The world urgently needs such committed builders of new paradigms of medical education."

CUBA'S HEALTH CARE REVOLUTION: 30 YEARS ON

Bulletin of the UN World Health Organization (WHO)
Volume 86, Number 5, May 2008

With the community-based polyclinic as its centre-piece, the country's primary health care system has produced enviable results as it continues to adapt to new challenges. Gail Reed reports from Havana.

"We fought for the Declaration of Alma-Ata before it was official," says Dr Cristina Luna, "and its message has guided and challenged us ever since." At 43, Luna is Cuba's national director of ambulatory care, and on her shoulders rests the country's entire primary health care system, by many standards one of the world's most effective and unique.

Cuban health authorities give large credit for the country's impressive health indicators to the prevent-ive, primary-care emphasis pursued for the last four decades. These indicators – which are close or equal to those in developed countries – speak for themselves. For example, in 2004, there were seven deaths for every 1000 children aged less than five years – a decrease from 46 such deaths 40 years earlier, according to WHO. Meanwhile Cubans have one of the world's highest life expectancies of 77 years.

The centrepiece of this system is the community-based polyclinic, each of the 498 nationwide serving a catchment area of between 30 000 and 60 000 people. The polyclinics act also as the organizational hub for 20 to 40 neighbourhood-based family doctor-and-nurse offices, and as accredited research and teaching centres for medical, nursing and allied health sciences students. "These are the backbone of Cuba's health system," Luna says.

"But today we're not just challenged to provide universal care at all levels, but also better quality care, better organized and integrated services. People expect much more of us now than when we were introducing the Rural Medical Service."

The period Luna refers to was the early 1960s, when Cuban government policy first focused on reaching people – mainly in rural areas – with little or no access to medical services following the Cuban revolution during the 1950s. The government started by enlisting 750 physicians and medical students for a period of their professional lives to work in the mountains and coastal communities. The aim of *el servicio médico rural* or the Rural Medical Service, according to its developers, was to provide "disease prevention and to revitalize health services for those most in need, whether because they are poor, in precarious health or live far from urban centres".

Multi-specialty polyclinics were established across Cuba in the 1970s, before the 1978 Declaration of Alma-Ata, and these were transformed with the addition of the family doctor-and-nurse programme in the mid-1980s, enhancing the health system's ability to deliver on prevention and community-health analysis, as well as clinical services. By the 1990s, the programme had posted family doctors and nurses throughout the country, and was attending to more than 95% of the population. "We were conscious that prevention had to be a cornerstone of our system," Luna says, "and that people had to be understood in all their dimensions: biological, psychological and social [and] as individuals, within families, and within their communities."

Today, Cuba has about 33 000 family physicians. Specialization in family medicine is a requirement for more than 97% of medical graduates, who spend one internship year and two residency years in training after they receive their degrees. Later, they can apply for a residency in a second specialty. As a result, the ranks in these second specialties are being swelled by physicians who started their careers in family medicine.

In 2008, Cuba's primary health care is again being transformed. Since 2002, 241 polyclinics have undergone extensive renovation, a process that continues today. The aim is to add services previously available only in hospitals. Now, the average polyclinic offers 22 services, including rehabilitation, X-ray, ultrasound, optometry, endoscopy, thrombolysis, emergency services, traumatology, clinical laboratory, family planning, emergency dentistry, maternal–child care, immunization, and diabetic and elderly care. Various other specialties – including dermatology, psychiatry and cardiology – are available too, in addition to family and internal medicine, paediatrics, and obstetrics and gynaecology.

Five-year-old Daysel Rojas has been attending the 5 de Septiembre Polyclinic in Havana for physiotherapy since he was four months' old. "The rehabilitation facilities are much broader now," says his mother, Dania Esquijarosa. "It makes a big difference to us, since we come every day. We don't have to wait, and they take the children first."

Dr Rebeca Mendoza, the director of the polyclinic, says 800 to 1000 patients a day use the services.

Another change has come with the abolition of a rather uniform type of polyclinic. "We once thought that each polyclinic should look the same," says Luna. "But a more rational and effective use of our resources says that beyond the polyclinics' basic set of services, additional ones should respond to the specific health picture of the community served. So, if there are many smokers, we should have counselling a few nights a week, not just one. If we have many allergies in the area, then the polyclinic should have allergy testing services, and so on."

This notion, in turn, relies on active population screening for a clear community health diagnosis. "We know from the family doctor-and-nurse surveys that we have 22.5% of people in our health area with high blood pressure," says Mendoza. "But we also know from national samplings that there are more who remain undiagnosed. Active screening allows us to take a particular condition, like hypertension, and look for the hidden prevalence."

The roles of the polyclinic and the family doctor-and-nurse offices are also changing. "Since 2007, the polyclinics are expected to play a leading role [in capacity building and quality control] among all health-related institutions in their communities," says Luna. "We bring the directors of the pharmacies, the elderly homes, the maternity homes and others into our team," adds Mendoza, "and we have also begun offering further training to the Federation of Cuban Women's health promoters, professionalizing their work in the community."

About half the family doctor-and-nurse offices are still headed by physicians; the other half by nurses whose work is guided by the family physician in the area. There are now about 2500 patients per physician-headed office at the primary care level, buttressed by these nurses who "have a greater role to play," says Luna. The new formula responds, in part, to the need to re-organize the system, with more than 20 000 Cuban physicians living abroad, mostly in Africa and Latin America. Training of new family physicians has also been put on the fast track: "We are now training some 42% more family doctors to make sure we have enough to meet all our commitments," says Luna.

What is left to address? Mendoza says: "We have to pay more attention to patient satisfaction. Some of the staff don't like to hear criticism. But I tell them, 'the day we think we're doing everything right is the day we've abandoned our patients, and also abandoned our commitment to the principles of Alma-Ata'."

HEALTH-WORKFORCE DEVELOPMENT IN THE CUBAN HEALTH SYSTEM

Miguel Márquez

Lancet Medical Journal *
Volume 374, Issue 9701, November 7, 2009

Health-workforce issues now receive much attention worldwide.[1] A well trained and well managed workforce is crucial for facilitating access to good-quality health services. Here I look at the Cuban experience in this area.

To support the development of the Cuban health system and achieve universal coverage, the training of physicians, nurses, and auxiliary personnel received priority attention after the 1959 revolution and continued in the decades after.[2,3] The number of medical and nursing schools and training centres for health technicians rapidly increased; the scope and depth of the training programmes were expanded to cover 24 specialties in addition to nursing; and measures were taken to expand the number of students and ensure their equitable distribution after graduation across the country. Medical education is free for students admitted to the training programmes after taking entrance exams.

Besides doctors and nurses, particular attention was placed on training auxiliary personnel (general, paediatric, and obstetric nursing auxiliaries) to serve in rural areas, and beginning in the mid-1970s, to health technicians, to meet the changing needs of the health system.

The development of a diversified health workforce has been crucial for the provision of free-of-charge services along the continuum of care, particularly ambulatory services in polyclinics, the basic unit of the system, staffed with doctors, nurses, and health technicians and serving a population of 25 000-30 000, and in specialised centres and at home.[4] Later in the mid-1980s, the system's community health-care approach was strengthened with the establishment of the Family Doctor Program, which has allowed the placement of a doctor trained in primary health care and a nurse in every neighbourhood (serving about 150 families).[4]

The sustained political priority on health-system development has had a positive impact, both in terms of the size and composition of the health workforce, and in the delivery of good-quality services with good health outcomes.[5] These achievements stand in contrast with the situation in countries with similar or higher per-capita incomes: Cuba's ratios for physicians and nurses at 63·4 and 83·8 per 10 000 population, respectively, are higher than in Argentina (33·4 and 2·2), Brazil (16·1 and 5·4), Chile (9·3 and 4·3), and even the United States (22·5 and 78·5).[6] Cuban health outcomes also match or surpass those in high-income countries, as reflected in low infant, child, and maternal mortality rates and a high healthy-life expectancy.[7]

Cuba's contribution to strengthening the health systems in other developing countries also merits highlighting.[8] This effort, which began in the 1960s, has helped to train health personnel from more than 108 countries. By 2007, more than 10 000 foreign students in all health professions had graduated after receiving free training under arrangements by the Government as part of bilateral relations with other countries. In recent years, the establishment of the Latin American School of Medicine in Havana has expanded the training of foreign doctors. By 2007, over 3000 foreign doctors had graduated from this school. Additionally, support has been provided for the establishment and operation of medical schools in 11 countries worldwide. Academic exchanges and collaborative activities have been done as well with universities in developed countries (eg, between Harvard Medical School's Department of Global Health and Social Medicine and the Pedro Kouri Institute of Tropical Medicine in Havana). The Medical Education Cooperation with Cuba (MEDICC), a non-profit organisation founded in 1997, is promoting interaction between the US, Cuban, and global health communities.[9]

The Cuban experience in the health sector seems to be a useful example of public policies that have prioritised development of human capital within a context of limited resources, and seems to have achieved good results. Cuban cooperation with other developing countries in the health sector is good international practice. Further funding from international agencies such as the Global Fund to Fight AIDS, Tuberculosis and Malaria, the GAVI Alliance, and the World Bank is necessary to support the scaling up of country collaborative efforts of this type and to reverse the deficits in human resources that hinder health-system strengthening in much of the developing world.[1,10]

I am a former PAHO/WHO Representative in Cuba (1989—96). I declare that I have no conflicts of interest.

References

1 - Vujici M, Ohiri K, Sparkes S. Working in health: financing and managing the public sector health workforce. http://www.who.intworkforcealliance/knowledge/publications/partner/workinginhealth_vujicic_worldbank_2009.pdf. (accessed Nov 1, 2009).

2 - De la Torre EE, Lopez C, Marquez M, Muniz G, Rojas F. Health for all is possible. Havana, Cuba: Cuban Public Health Society, 2005. (in Spanish).

3 - Hernández E, Marquez M. Medical education in Cuba. Educ Med Salud 1976; 10: 1-41. (in Spanish). PubMed

4 - World Bank. World development report 2004: making services work for

poor people. http://econ.worldbank.org/WBSITE/EXTERNAL/EXT-DEC/EXTRESEARCH/EXTWDRS/EXTWDR2004/0,,menuPK:477704/pagePK:64167702/piPK:64167676/theSitePK:477688,00.html. (accessed Nov 1, 2009).

5 - WHO. World health report: primary health care now more than ever. http://www.who.int/whr/2008/en/index.html. (accessed Nov 3, 2009).

6 - Pan American Health Organization. Health situation in the Americas: basic indicators. http://www.paho.org/English/DD/AIS/BI_2007_ENG.pdf. (accessed Nov 1, 2009).

7 - Pan American Health Organization. Health in the Americas. Vol II—countries, Cuba. http://www.paho.org/HIA/archivosvol2/paisesing/Cuba%20English.pdf. (accessed Nov 1, 2009).

8 - Marimon N, Martinez E. International health collaboration. La Habana, Cuba: OPS/OMS, 2009. (in Spanish).

9 - Cuban research in current international journals. MEDICC Rev Int J Cuban Health Med 2009; 11: 3. (abstr). PubMed

10 - WHO. World health report: working together for health. http://www.who.int/whr/2008/en/index.html. (accessed Nov 1, 2009).

a - Miramar, Havana, Cuba

Reprinted with permission.
The Lancet is one of the world's leading medical journals. The British publication was founded in 1923, and is independent, without affiliation to a medical or scientific organisation. The Lancet publishes medical news, research and articles related to public health.

THE RIGHT TO HEALTH IN TIMES OF ECONOMIC CRISIS: CUBA'S WAY

Pol de Vos, Patrick Van der Stuyft

Lancet Medical Journal *
Volume 374, Issue 9701, November 7, 2009

The current economic crisis affects the health of millions of people in developing countries and palliative sectorial aid is needed.[1] By contrast, Cuba's economy has been in crisis for almost 20 years—since the Soviet Union's breakdown followed by a tightened US embargo—without much impact, at least on health outcomes.[2,3] Why?

After the 1959 Cuban revolution, the Government tackled socioeconomic health determinants with redistributive policies, developed participation structures, and set up a comprehensive health system. Equitable policies, in line with what we call today a health-rights approach, were stubbornly, but successfully, sustained after 1990. The health-care system guarantees accessible, integrated, and effective curative services and stresses prevention. The different levels of care interact adequately. Balanced development of resources led to a dense network of facilities, from the doctor's cabinet in the neighbourhood to the university hospital, with the essential technology, comfortable staff-population ratios (63·4 physicians and 83·8 nurses per 10 000 inhabitants[3]), and local production of diagnostics and drugs (covering 85% of the needs, including antiretrovirals and cytostatics).[4]

The tenet of Cuba's exclusively public system is the first line of defence, in which the family doctor has had a central role since the 1980s. He or she serves a well-defined population for which the doctor functions as the entry point to and coach through the system. Family doctors and nurses also analyse ecological risks within the community and the perceived health problems of the population in their area.[5] This permits fine-tuning of curative and preventive activities and the setting of local priorities for intersectorial action.

A comprehensive research policy supports the health sector's development. Operational research ranges from optimising use of care[6] to strengthening community-based disease control.[7] Biotechnology research led to novel diagnostic tools and recombinant vaccines against hepatitis B, meningitis B, and *Haemophilus influenzae* type b.[8] Close links between research institutes and health policy makers ensure the swift introduction of innovations in the local health system, and in international solidarity programmes. Cuba develops supplies that are instrumental in controlling health problems it does not face itself, besides sending over 30 000 health professionals abroad and training similar numbers of young foreign students.[9]

Can these achievements be preserved? Equitable distribution of consumer goods and services has been under strain since the 1990s. In the health sector, periodic shortages of drugs opened a niche for a black market and waiting lists for interventions triggered informal coping mechanisms.[10] The decreased availability and rapid turnover of family doctors—a consequence of intensified international collaboration since 2004—also constitutes a challenge. Concurrently, Cuba's ageing population is in need of more and better organised management for chronic diseases and psychosocial care. Moreover, due to the current global crisis, export earnings dropped dramatically in 2008 and tourism revenues decreased.

As Raùl Castro recently reminded us, "Nobody can indefinitely spend more than he earns. Two plus two is four, never five. Moreover, in the conditions of our imperfect socialism, because of our own insufficiencies, many times two plus two results to be three".[11] Specific measures, such as higher wages and targeted welfare to gradually substitute for free and subsidised goods, are now being publicly debated nationwide. However, the state's core functions that ensure the population's wellbeing—education, health care, and social security—remain unchallenged political priorities, which budget allocations will continue to reflect.[11] At sectorial level, plans made to strengthen the role of the family doctor and nurse as a coordinating hub in an integrated health and social system seem the correct way forward.[12] To compensate for the health personnel sent abroad, training of human resources is being accelerated. Nevertheless, they need to be more stably stationed in the community.

From a human-rights perspective, Cuba's response to economic crisis exemplifies the role that a developing country state can play to ensure its citizens' health: tackle all socioeconomic determinants of health and embed sectorial health measures in a redistributive intersectorial policy. The determination of Cuba's Government to assume responsibility to protect and develop its citizens' right to health seems intact. The international community could assist by increasing pressure to make the USA revoke the crippling embargo.

Since 1996 both authors have participated in research activities with Cuban institutes affiliated to the Ministry of Health.

References

1 - World Bank. Crisis hitting poor hard in developing world, World Bank says. http://go.worldbank.org/PGNOX87VO0. (accessed Oct 29, 2009).

2 - Cooper RS, Kennelly JF, Orduñez-Garcia P. Health in Cuba. Int J Epidemiol 2006; 35: 817-824. CrossRef|PubMed

3 - Pan American Health Organization. Health Information and Analysis Project.

Health situation in the Americas: basic indicators 2009.http://new.paho.org/hq/ index.php?option=com_docman&task=doc_download&gid=3050&Itemid. (accessed Nov 3, 2009).

4 - De Vos P. Health report on Cuba. "No one left abandoned": Cuba's national health system since the 1959 revolution. Int J Health Serv 2005; 35: 189-207. CrossRef|PubMed

5 - Eisen G. Primary care in Cuba: the family doctor team and the polyclinic. La atención primaria en Cuba: el equipo del médico de la familia y el policlínico. Rev Cub Salud Pub 1996; 22: 117-124. (in Spanish). PubMed

6 - De Vos P, Murlá P, Rodriguez A, Bonet M, Más P, Van der Stuyft P. Shifting the demand for emergency care in Cuba's health system. Soc Sci Med 2005; 60: 609-616. CrossRef|PubMed

7 - Toledo-Romani ME, Vanlerberghe V, Perez D, et al. Achieving sustainability of community-based dengue control in Santiago de Cuba. Soc Sci Med 2007; 64: 976-988. CrossRef|PubMed

8 - Lage A. Connecting immunology research to public health: Cuban biotechnology. Nature 2008; 9: 109-112. PubMed

9 - De Vos P, De Ceukelaire W, Bonet M, Van der Stuyft P. Cuba's international cooperation in health: an overview. Int J Health Serv 2007; 37: 761-776. CrossRef|PubMed

10 - Jenkins TM. Patients, practitioners, and paradoxes: responses to the Cuban health crisis of the 1990s. Qual Health Res 2008; 18: 1384-1400. CrossRef|PubMed

11 - Castro R. The people, with its party in the vanguard, must decide. Speech at the National Assembly. http://www.granma.cubaweb.cu/2009/08/01/nacional/ artic19.html. (accessed Oct 29, 2009) (in Spanish).

12 - WHO. The world health report 2008. Primary health care: now more than ever. http://www.who.int/whr/2008/en/index.html. (accessed Oct 29, 2009).

a - Institute of Tropical Medicine, 2000 Antwerp, Belgium

Reprinted with permission.
The Lancet is one of the world's leading medical journals. The British publication was founded in 1923, and is independent, without affiliation to a medical or scientific organisation. The Lancet publishes medical news, research and articles related to public health.

Role of the USA in Shortage of Food and Medicine in Cuba

Anthony F. Kirkpatrick, MD,

Lancet Medical Journal*
Volume 348, Issue 9040, November 30, 1996

For over 30 years an embargo by the USA has restricted Cuba's ability to purchase foods and medicines. In 1992, the USA enacted the Cuban Democracy Act (CDA), which "exempted" the sale of medicines from the embargo. However, the implementation of the CDA's requirements and the intensification of the embargo as a result of the passage of the Helms-Burton Act in March, 1996, have undermined the purpose of the medicine exemption. The resultant lack of food and medicine to Cuba contributed to the worst epidemic of neurological disease this century. The Inter-American Commission on Human Rights of the Organization of American States has informed the US Government that such activities violate international law and has requested that the US take immediate steps to exempt food and medicine from the embargo.

Health professionals need to understand how an economic embargo of a country can have a direct, negative effect on its public health. The US embargo against Cuba is unprecedented because it imposes restrictions on the sale of medicine and food. Indeed, the Clinton Administration described the Cuban embargo as "the most comprehensive embargo the United States has against any country in the World".[1]

My aim was to determine to what extent recent US Government policies contribute to a shortage of medicines and medical equipment in Cuba, and how. The data were gathered from telephone conversations, records, and written communications obtained between 1993 and 1996. It should be noted that some of the participants in this survey did not want their cooperation to be construed as taking a position on any US Government agency or US policy.

US Jurisdiction Over Medical Products

The USA has immense control over the availability of essential drugs worldwide. The figure [next page] shows that the US pharmaceutical industry has a significant global lead in the discovery and development of major drugs. The US monopoly spans almost all therapeutic and diagnostic applications.[2,3]

Development of 265 major global drugs from 1970 to May, 1992, by national origin

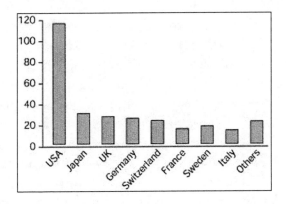

"Major global drugs" must have been marketed or have reached the post-clinical stage in at least 6 of 7 of the world's leading markets: the USA, Japan, Germany, France, Italy, the UK, and Spain. A presence in 6 or 7 markets requires the inclusion of at least two or three leading continents, and acceptance by various medical cultures. "National origin" is the nationality of the originating company, or the parent to which the originator belonged at the time of market introduction. Data adapted from ref 2.

For over 30 years an embargo by the US has restricted Cuba's access to these essential medicines.[4] However, with the tightening of the embargo in 1992 through the passage of the Cuban Democracy Act (CDA) many of these medicines became virtually unattainable. The new restrictions required that the President of the USA certify, through on-site inspections approved by the President, that all components of a shipment of medical products to Cuba were used for the purpose intended.[5] The US Government knew that it could not do these on-site inspections. The US Government therefore shifted the burden of on-site inspections to the exporters. The manufacturers had to accept the responsibility for verifying the end use of each product sold to Cuba, at an increased administrative cost. If certain procedures were not followed, the manufacturers could be subject to penalties of up to $1 million per violation for corporations and prison terms up to 10 years for individuals. The Cuban Government has allowed some of these on-site inspections, even though it intrudes on Cuba's sovereignty.

The US Government, for its part, seems to make a concerted effort to frustrate medical companies attempting to export goods to Cuba. For example, Johnson & Johnson was forced to wait a year to receive an export licence.[6] Other companies have found the licence-application process insurmountable, even for the sale of $200 of replacement parts for radiographic equipment (Cody N, Picker International, Cleveland, Ohio, USA; personal communication). According to Iris Medical, an international supplier of ophthalmological equipment, "Despite a substantial expenditure of time and resources, Iris Medical was unable to establish a meaningful dialog with the US Department of Commerce in a manner consistent with standard business practices" (Arias E, Iris Medical, Mountain View, California, USA; personal communication). Even WHO is subject to the CDA restrictions.[6] Consequently, as the table shows, only a few of the world's medical companies have attempted to brave US regulations since the enactment of the CDA. The number of companies granted US licences to sell to Cuba has fallen to less than 4% of pre-CDA levels.[4] *(See table on page 132).*

US License Applications For Sale Of Medical Products To Cuba

The largest pharmaceutical firm in the USA, Merck, announced on Dec 19, 1995, that it will never do business with Cuba while the embargo is in place. Merck was prosecuted by the US Government for an exchange of scientific information with Cuba. Merck described the exchange of information as an opportunity to assist WHO in its Pan-American health-care activities. There was no commercial transaction. Merck reports that they believed that they had a "gentleman's agreement" with the US Department of Treasury to keep a low profile about the incident (Bearse S, Merck, Whitehouse, New Jersey, USA; personal communication). However, when President Fidel Castro came to New York City in October, 1995, to attend the United Nations' 50th anniversary celebration, the US Treasury Department publicized the Merck incident.[7] Similarly,

US agency (product and origin)	Product use	Applicant	Date	Approval
Treasury department				
Cytometer (UK)	Blood analysis	Johnson & Johnson	June 16, 1993	Yes
Thalamonal (Belgium)	Analgesia	Johnson & Johnson	June 3, 1993; Feb 18, 1994; Sept 2, 1994	Yes
Fluspirilene (Belgium)	Antipsychotic	Johnson & Johnson	Feb 25, 1994	Yes
Syringes (Belgium)	Drug injection	Beckton Dickinson	March 7, 1994	Yes
Depo-Provera (Belgium)	Contraception	Upjohn	Dec 1, 1993; Aug 17, 1994	Yes
Commerce department				
Ventilator parts (Sweden)	Replacement parts	Sieman	July, 1994	Yes
Radiographic equipment (Canada)	Replacement parts	Picker	April 29, 1994	Denied
Photocoagulator (USA)	Eye disorders	Iris Medical	Oct 1, 1993	Denied

Documents obtained through the Freedom of Information Act; request to the Office of Foreign Asset Control of the US Department of Treasury, Aug 27, 1996. Data also obtained by the author from the licensee.

Table: **US licence applications for sale of medical products to Cuba** when International Murex Technologies of the USA acquired a diagnostics company from the UK, Murex banned the sale of diagnostic products from the UK to Cuba for fear of reprisals by the US Government and the risk of adverse publicity (Ramsey S, International Murex Corporation, Norcross, Georgia, USA; personal communication). As a result, Cuba had to find a new supplier of diagnostic products followed by 3—6 months of validation testing in Cuba before some of the products could be used.

Merck's and Murex's experiences with the Cuban embargo are only examples of other US-induced barriers and deterrents for trade in medical products with Cuba. These include fear of huge financial penalties and imprisonment of company employees, increased legal costs, US Government prosecution for minor and inadvertent violations of the Cuban embargo, and follow-up solicitation of the press for adverse publicity against the medical company and its employees.

Non-US Medical-Product Companies

The US embargo imposes significant restrictions on Cuba acquiring non-US products. For example, foreign vessels are banned from loading or unloading freight anywhere in the US for at least 6 months after having stopped in Cuba. Similarly, aircraft carrying emergency medical supplies to Cuba are banned from landing in the USA (which creates delays).

The Helms-Burton Act, which was passed in March, 1996, is having an inhibiting effect on non-US medical companies. For example, the Act instructs US officials to bar US entry to "any alien"—non-US medical company directors as well as their families and children—who "traffics" in American property that was confiscated by the Cuban government after the 1959 takeover by Fidel Castro.[8] Another provision would allow US citizens to sue such firms—ie, those trafficking in nationalized properties, in US courts. President Clinton has postponed the implementation of the latter provision until Jan 15, 1997. But even if he renews the suspension of the lawsuit part of the Act, the law will remain on the books and serve as a disincentive to companies that may wish to sell medicines to Cuba. What makes the current law so difficult to change is the way it came into effect in March. In a major concession to the Republican-controlled Congress, Clinton relinquished some of his authority as President over foreign affairs and agreed that the only way the Act could be amended or overturned is by another act of Congress. It is unsurprising that Mexico, Canada, and the European Union are threatening to retaliate if the USA tries to punish them.

For Cuba, the costs of medical products have increased because the country has few potential suppliers, and therefore little negotiating strength. Cubans complain that non-US medical companies raise prices because of increased transportation costs and increased risk due to possible reprisals from the US Government. The effect on Cuba's health system is increased costs, shipping delays, and restricted access to some of the most important medical products because they are subject to US jurisdiction.

In February, 1995, a group of concerned US citizens, including me, approached the Inter-American Commission on Human Rights of the Organization of American States (OAS) to point out that the inclusion of foods and medicines in the US trade embargo against Cuba was a violation of common international law. The matter was discussed at hearings at the OAS that month and the Commission—in a little-noticed letter—urged the US Government to end restrictions on shipment of food and medicines to Cuba, calling them a violation of international law.[9] This development was significant because the OAS has excluded Cuba from membership of the organization. In addition, the OAS was one of the first international organizations to deplore violations of human rights by the Fidel Castro's Government.

In response to the opinion of the OAS, the USA maintains that medicines and medical supplies are exempt from the US embargo and can be sold to Cuba. The USA insists, however, that it must be able to verify their proper distribution.[10] This provision, and the other bureaucratic requirements implemented by the US Government, effectively subverts the medical-supply exception to the embargo. In essence, the USA remains in violation of international law.

Food And The Future

The US Government acknowledges that there is no exemption for food items; it simply notes that there are "ample suppliers" of foodstuffs elsewhere, that Cuba receives donations of food, and that the food shortages are not due to the embargo, but, rather, are caused by the "Regime's failure to alter Cuba's inefficient centralized economic system".[10]

This argument rings hollow. First, even if Cuba can buy food elsewhere, the inclusion of food in the US trade embargo remains in violation of international law. Second, a small amount of food is donated by US organisations,[4,10] but that is a poor substitute for removing provisions that prohibit its sale. Third, although Cuba can buy food elsewhere, it must often pay higher transportation costs than would be the case with the nearby USA. Fourth, in 1992, the US Government ignored the warning of the American Public Health Association that the tightening of the embargo would lead to an abrupt cessation of supplies of food and medicine to Cuba resulting in widespread "famines".[4] In fact, 5 months after the passage of the Act the worst epidemic of neurological disease this century due to a food shortage became widespread in Cuba.[12] More than 50 000 of the 11 million inhabitants were suffering from optic neuropathy, deafness, loss of sensation and pain in the extremities, and a spinal disorder that impaired walking and bladder control.[11,13] Furthermore, as recently as November, 1995, WHO reported more people with neurological disease in Cuba due to malnutrition.[14]

In June, 1993, a delegation sponsored by the American Public Health Association travelled to Cuba to assess the impact of the embargo on the public health of the Cuban people. The Association's report notes that the policies of the Castro regime give a high priority for health care, which has contributed to a large reduction in infant mortality and improvements in health. However, the Association found that the tightening US embargo, through the enactment of the CDA, has been associated with a decline in the health of the Cuban people.[15]

The US Government often speaks of violations of human rights in Cuba. Such claims should perhaps be viewed against the background of an Amnesty International report, which catalogues human-rights abuses in the USA, such as torture, ill-treatment of prisoners, and excessive use of force by police.[16] In addition, it should be noted that Washington has been deemed to have exaggerated Cuba's abuses of human rights, to the extent of codifying such claims into US law.[17] These reports should be borne in mind when the US blockade of food and medicine to Cuba is considered.

I thank Victor Sidel, Robert Miller, Wayne Smith, and Robert Bedford for their help with this study and in

the preparation of this report.

References

1 - Carter T. Aid sees embargo over if Cuba reforms. Washington Times July 30, 1995. PubMed

2 - Redwood H. Price regulation and pharmaceutical research. Felixstowe, Suffolk, UK: Oldwicks Press, 1994.

3 - Pharmaceutical Research and Manufacturers of America. World class drugs: origin of 97 "globalized" drugs 1975—1989. Washington, DC: Pharmaceutical Research and Manufacturers of America, 1994. Citin PE Barral. Fifteen years of results of pharmaceutical research in the world. Paris: Perspective et Sante Publique, 1990.

4 - In: US Senate hearing before the subcommittee on western hemisphere and peace corps affairs. Washington DC: Government Printing Office, Aug 5, 1992: 44-116.

5 - Cuban Democracy Act appears at title XVII 1993 National Defense Authorization Act, Oct 23, 1992.

6 - Kirkpatrick A. Medicine and the US embargo against Cuba. JAMA 1996; 275: 1633-1637. PubMed

7 - Embargo violations cost drug maker. USA Today, Oct 25, 1995: 3A.

8 - Helms-Burton Act, Pub L No. 104—114, March 12, 1996.

9 - Walte J, US urged to ease Cuban embargo. USA Today. March 7. 1995.

10 - United States Permanent Mission of the Organization of American States. ARA press guidance; Cuba: position of Inter—American Commission on Human Rights. Washington, DC: United States Permanent Mission to the Organization of American States, March 3, 1995.

11 - The Cuba Neuropathy field Investigation Team. Epidemic optic neuropathy in Cuba: clinical characterization and risk factors. N Engl J Med 1995; 333: 1176-1182. CrossRef | PubMed

12 - Roman GC. Epidemic neuropathy in Cuba: a plea to end the United States economic embargo on a humanitarian basis. Neurology 1994; 44: 1784-1786.

PubMed

13 - Roman GC. On politics and health: an epidemic of neurologic disease in Cuba. Ann Intern Med 1995; 122: 530-533. PubMed

14 - Monmaney T, Politics of an epidemic. *Los Angeles Times.* Nov 20, 1995.

15 - American Public Health Association. The politics of suffering: the impact of the US embargo on the health of the Cuban people. Washington DC: American Public Health Association, 1993.

16 - Amnesty International. United States of America: human rights violations: a summary of Amnesty International's concerns. London, UK: Amnesty International, 1995.

17 - Human Rights Watch/Americas. Cuba: improvements without reform. Washington, DC: Human Rights Watch/Americas, 1995.

* Reprinted with permission.
The Lancet is one of the world's leading medical journals. The British publication was founded in 1923, and is independent, without affiliation to a medical or scientific organisation. The Lancet publishes medical news, research and articles related to public health.

MAPS

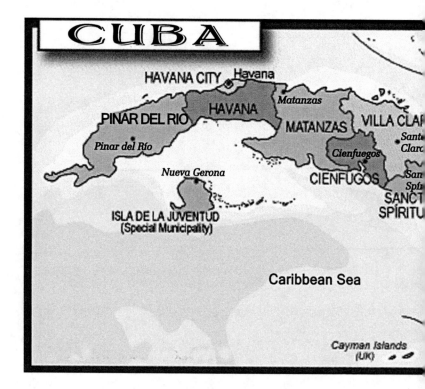

142

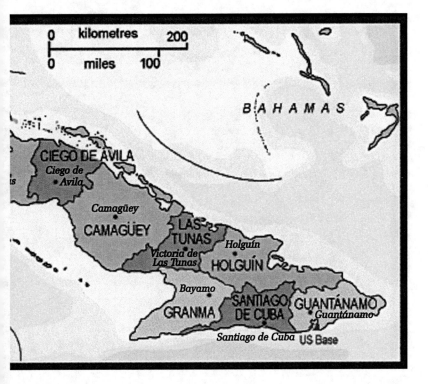

143

Cuba, the Caribbean and the Americas

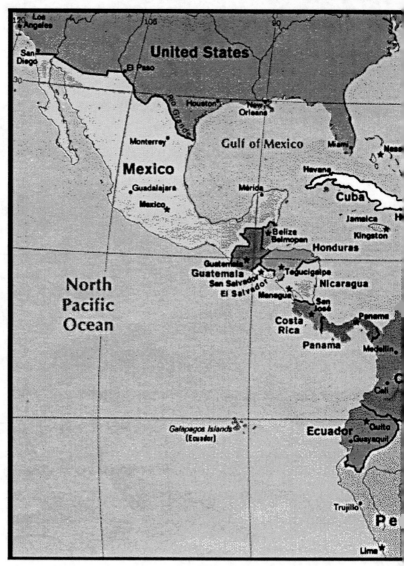

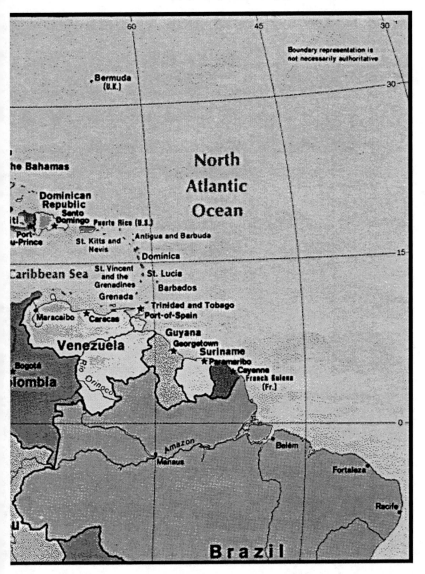

145

Americas

1 - Antigua & Barbuda
2 - Argentina
3 - Aruba
4 - Bahamas
5 - Belize
6 - Bolivia
7 - Brazil
8 - Chile
9 - Colombia
10 - Costa Rica
11 - Dominica
12 - Dominican Republic
13 - Dutch Antilles Bonaire
14 - Ecuador
15 - El Salvador
16 - Guatemala
17 - Guyana
18 - Grenada
19 - Haiti
20 - Honduras
21 - Jamaica
22 - Mexico
23 - Panama
24 - Paraguay
25 - Peru
26 - St Lucia
27 - St Kitts & Nevis
28 - St. Vincent & the Grenadines
29 - Surinam
30 - Trinidad & Tobago
31 - United States of America
32 - Venezuela

146

Health Assistance in 2002

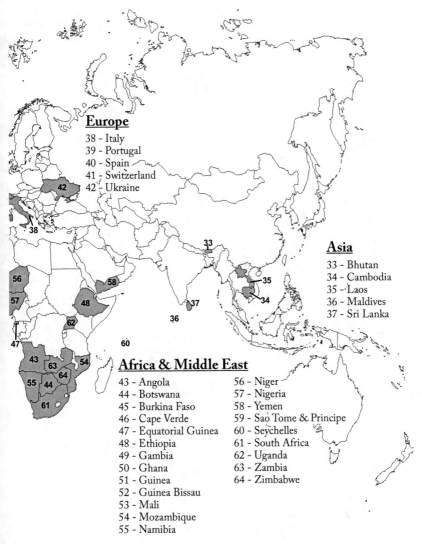

Europe
38 - Italy
39 - Portugal
40 - Spain
41 - Switzerland
42 - Ukraine

Asia
33 - Bhutan
34 - Cambodia
35 - Laos
36 - Maldives
37 - Sri Lanka

Africa & Middle East
43 - Angola
44 - Botswana
45 - Burkina Faso
46 - Cape Verde
47 - Equatorial Guinea
48 - Ethiopia
49 - Gambia
50 - Ghana
51 - Guinea
52 - Guinea Bissau
53 - Mali
54 - Mozambique
55 - Namibia

56 - Niger
57 - Nigeria
58 - Yemen
59 - Sao Tome & Principe
60 - Seychelles
61 - South Africa
62 - Uganda
63 - Zambia
64 - Zimbabwe

Cuba and International Medical Education:

For the 2006-2007 academic year, there were 30,777 forei *scholarship students in Cuba. They came from 126 countries ar* *81% were enrolled in medical programmes, both at ELAM ar* *other medical institutions.*

Cuba has also assisted in establishing medical schools around t *world, in countries such as Paraguay, Guyana, Guinea Bissa* *the Gambia, Equatorial Guinea and Yemen.*

Americas

1 - Argentina
2 - Belize
3 - Bolivia
4 - Brazil
5 - Chile
6 - Colombia
7 - Costa Rica
8 - Dominican Republic
9 - Ecuador
10 - El Salvador
11 - Guatemala
12 - Haiti
13 - Honduras
14 - Jamaica
15 - Mexico
16 - Nicaragua
17 - Panama
18 - Paraguay
19 - Peru
20 - St Kitts & Nevis
21 - United States of America
22 - Uruguay
23 - Venezuela

STUDYING IN CUBA AT THE
OF MEDICINE - ELAM

Facts on the Latin American School of Medicine:

Students from more countries than represented on this map are currently studying at the Latin American School of Medicine (ELAM). There are currently students from 55 countries studying at ELAM and students from over 88 countries (including Canada) on scholarship studying at other medical schools in Cuba.

As of March 2010, there are approximately 10,000 students at ELAM and there has been 5 graduations with a total of 7,248 graduates. 75 percent of the students come from farmer and worker's families. Many different ethnic groups are represented, including 104 aboriginal communities of Latin America. In 2006, 51 percent of students were women.

The foreign scholarship program at ELAM includes full tuition, dormitory housing, three meals per day at the campus cafeteria, textbooks in Spanish for all courses, school uniforms, basic toiletries, bedding, and a small monthly stipend.

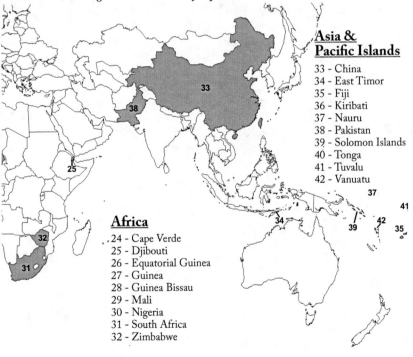

Asia &
Pacific Islands

33 - China
34 - East Timor
35 - Fiji
36 - Kiribati
37 - Nauru
38 - Pakistan
39 - Solomon Islands
40 - Tonga
41 - Tuvalu
42 - Vanuatu

Africa

24 - Cape Verde
25 - Djibouti
26 - Equatorial Guinea
27 - Guinea
28 - Guinea Bissau
29 - Mali
30 - Nigeria
31 - South Africa
32 - Zimbabwe

Also Available from Battle of Ideas Press

WAR AND OCCUPATION IN AFGHANISTAN WHICH WAY FORWARD?

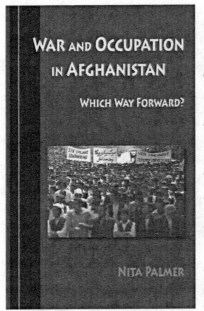

"The problem of Afghanistan boils down to just two words: foreign occupation. The Canada/US/NATO occupation forces claim that corruption, poverty, drug production, the presence of the Taliban and other social or political crises are the fundamental problems of Afghanistan which they must fix. The irony of this claim is that the same occupation forces have proven themselves completely incapable of fixing these problems or of bettering the lives of Afghan people one bit after eight years of occupation. Under the watchful eye of the occupation forces, corruption has become rampant in Afghanistan, from the local level all the way up to the highest levels of government. Afghanistan has gone from producing less than 10% of the world's opium in 2001 to producing a staggering 93% of the world's opium in 2008, according to the UN World Health Organization."

BY NITA PALMER

Nita Palmer is an author and researcher on the war in Afghanistan. She is a member of the editorial board of Vancouver, Canada-based social justice newspaper Fire This Time and the secretary of Mobilization Against War and Occupation.

January 2010, paperback, 155 pages, illustrated, $7.00
ISBN 978-0-9864716-0-5 | Copyright © 2010 by Battle of Ideas Press
PO Box 21607, Vancouver, BC, V5L 5G3, Canada
WWW.BATTLEOFIDEASPRESS.COM | INFO@BATTLEOFIDEASPRESS.COM

Also Available from Battle of Ideas Press

5 Decades of the Cuban Revolution
The Challenges of an Unwavering Leadership

"The battles Cuba has fought have not been easy. Some were physical battles, such as the battle against bandits in the Escambray Mountains or the Bay of Pigs invasion. However, most were not battles of physical might, but battles of ideas. But with every twist and turn, every up and down Fidel has been one of the first leaders to say, 'this way forward' or 'we made a wrong turn, we must change course."

By Tamara Hansen

Tamara Hansen is an co-chair and an executive committee member of the Canadian Network on Cuba (CNC). She is also an editorial board member of Fire This Time newspaper. She has travelled to Cuba nine times and has written extensively on Cuban politics since 2003.

April 2010, paperback, 312 pages, illustrated, $10.00
ISBN 978-0-9864716-1-2 | Copyright © 2010 by Battle of Ideas Press
PO Box 21607, Vancouver, BC, V5L 5G3, Canada
WWW.BATTLEOFIDEASPRESS.COM | INFO@BATTLEOFIDEASPRESS.COM

Coming Soon from Battle of Ideas Press

Resisting Colonialism: The Indigenous Struggle for Self-Determination
By Aaron Mercredi

Che Guevara, Thinker and Fighter: Selected Writings and Speeches

Prisoners of the Empire: The Case of the 5 Cuban Heroes

Volveran! A Collection of Poetry in Honour of the Cuban 5

Canada: Peacekeeper or War Maker?

PO Box 21607, Vancouver, BC, V5L 5G3, Canada
WWW.BATTLEOFIDEASPRESS.COM | INFO@BATTLEOFIDEASPRESS.COM